Abstract

The purpose of this monograph is to give an overview and a discussion of some recent results about computational complexity of feasible computations and the study of provable properties about complexity of computations. In the first part we concentrate on the relations between complete sets under log n-tape reductions of such natural families of languages as *NL*, *CSL*, *P*, *NP* and *PTAPE* and results about their structure.

In the last part, we consider what can and cannot be proven formally about complexity of computations and show that some of the well known results in computational complexity change their character considerably if we demand that the complexity properties under consideration must be formally verifiable. We conclude by a discussion of the possibility that the famous $P = NP$? problem could be independent of the axioms of set theory.

Acknowledgments

This monograph is based on lectures delivered at the NSF supported Regional Conference on Feasible Computations, January 3–8, 1977, at Texas A&M University, Lubbock, Texas. The preparation of this monograph has been supported in part by National Science Foundation under Grant DCR75-09433.

Contents

CHAPTER 1

Introduction

During the last half a dozen years computational complexity has been strongly influenced and advanced by the investigation of *efficient reductions* between problems and problem classes. In particular, the study of the deterministic and nondeterministic polynomial time computations, *P* and *NP*, revealed the existence of "natural" complete problems in the class *NP* to which all other problems in this class can be efficiently reduced. Furthermore, it was shown that many problems of practical importance are contained in the class *NP* and that many of these problems are complete, thus showing, quite surprisingly, that a fast algorithm for any one of these (complete) problems can be effectively translated into fast algorithms for all other problems in this class [11], [31].

Subsequent research on feasible computations has progressed very rapidly and has shown that there exist rich structural relations, revealed by efficient reductions, between different classes of computations, and it has increased our understanding feasible computations quite dramatically. As a matter of fact, this work has revealed a deep unity of this research area and has identified several super problems whose solution seems to be essential for a complete understanding of the structure of feasible computations. Thus these results have not only added to our understanding of the quantitative aspect of computing but have also unified a central field of research in computer science and are very likely to strongly influence its further development by creating a consensus about what problems are important and should be thoroughly investigated [1], [11], [24], [25], [31], [41].

It may only be a slight exaggeration to claim that in the 1930s we started to understand what is and is not *effectively* computable and that in the 1970s we started to understand what is and is not *practically* or *feasibly* computable. There is no doubt that the results about what can and cannot be effectively computed or formalized in mathematics have had a profound influence on mathematics, and, even more broadly, they have influenced our view of our scientific methods. We believe that the results about what can and cannot be practically computed will also have a major influence on computer science, mathematics and, even though more slowly, will affect other research areas and influence how we think about scientific theories.

The purpose of this monograph is to give an overview of some of the more recent developments in the study of the structure of feasible computations and in the investigation of provable properties of complexity of computations and their relations to feasible computations. This monograph treats only a select set of topics trying to show some of the techniques of this research, giving some insight into the results and emphasizing the unity of this research area.

In the first part of the monograph we define and discuss efficient reductions between problems and consider such families of languages as *NL*, *DCSL*, *CSL*, *P*, *NP*, *PTAPE*, *EXPTIME* and *EXPTAPE* and the corresponding complete languages. All through this study we use log n-tape bounded reductions which are seen to be a subset of the often used and extensively studied polynomial-time reductions, though at the present it is not known whether the log n-tape reductions form a proper subset of the polynomial time reductions [1], [21], [28]–[31]. The use of log n-tape reductions permit us to extend in a uniform way our definitions and results to the computationally simpler natural families of languages, such as *NL*, *P* and *CSL*, to which the polynomial time reductions did not apply (or, as in the case of *CSL*, were not known to apply) [21], [28]–[31]. We show that all the "known" complete languages of *NL*, *CSL*, *P*, *NP*, *PTAPE*, etc. are, respectively, log n-tape isomorphic. Thus we show that despite the great variety and different origins of complete problems for the above discussed families of languages, they all are respectively, very similar in a strong technical sense [21]. This extends and strengthens the previously known results about polynomial time isomorphism of complete sets in *NP*, *PTAPE*, etc. [3], [4], [5].

We also show that complete sets in *DCSL*, *CSL*, *PTAPE* and in computationally more complex families of languages cannot be sparse. As a matter of fact we show that complete sets in these families cannot be log n-tape reduced to any sparse set (recursive or otherwise), thus showing that there is no sparse amount of information which can be utilized by means of log n-tape computations to aid in computing complete sets in the above families [3], [4], [21].

Furthermore, we consider the existence of easy to recognize infinite subsets in complete sets. In particular we show that any complete set for the family of (deterministic) context-sensitive languages must contain infinite subsets which are log n-tape acceptable. The same result also holds for *CSL*, *PTAPE* and computationally more complex families of languages [3], [21].

By similar methods we give an easy proof that any recognition method of a creative set can be effectively speeded up by arbitrary large amounts on infinite subsets. This shows, among other things, that any axiomatizable formal mathematical system (in which we can prove elementary facts about Turing machines) must contain infinite subsets of trivially true (easily recognizable) theorems whose proofs in the formal system are arbitrarily long. Thus every proof system for sufficiently rich mathematical theories can be effectively replaced by another one which yields much simpler proofs on an infinite set of theorems, to whose triviality the first proof system is blind [8], [19].

In the last part of this monograph we consider the problem of what can and cannot be proven formally about running times of algorithms and relate this problem to the problem of establishing sharp time bounds for one-tape Turing machine computations [18], [20]. We also relate the existence of gaps in the hierarchy of complexity classes to the inability to prove running times for algorithms formally by showing that we can have a gap in the hierarchy only if the classic complexity class properly contains the corresponding provable complexity class [20]. Furthermore, we show that for provably equivalent programs certain optimality (speed-up) properties are independent of the function computed and depend only on the representation of the given program [44]. These results suggest very strongly that we need to explore further how our "world view" of the complexity of algorithms has to be changed if we consider only provable properties of algorithms.

We conclude by considering the possibility that the classic

$$P = NP?$$

problem may be independent of the axioms of formal mathematical systems, such as formal set theory [23].

CHAPTER 2

Reductions and Complete Sets

It is well known from recursive function theory that there exist complete recursively enumerable sets to which any other recursively enumerable (r.e.) set can be reduced by recursive mappings [38]. Thus these complete r.e. sets are in a strict technical sense "universal" or "hardest" among all recursively enumerable sets and they characterize what is effectively computable. Let

$$M_1, M_2, M_3, \ldots$$

be a standard enumeration of Turing machines (Tm), and let

$$L(M_i)$$

denote the language accepted by the machine M_i. Then an example of a complete r.e. set is given by

$$U = \{(M_i, w) | M_i \text{ accepts input } w\}.$$

It is easily seen that U is an r.e. set and that for any Tm M_{i_0} the recursive mapping σ, given by

$$\sigma(w) = (M_{i_0}, w),$$

is such that

$$w \in L(M_{i_0}) \quad \text{iff} \quad \sigma(w) = (M_{i_0}, w) \in U.$$

Thus we see that any r.e. set can be reduced to U by a recursive mapping. Though the proof that U is a complete r.e. set follows almost immediately from the existence of universal Turing machines, the set U may appear somewhat artificially constructed. On the other hand, it is not difficult to prove that there exist "natural" complete r.e. sets which play a very important role in mathematics. As a matter of fact, the set of all provable theorems in formalized set theory or formalized number theory form complete r.e. sets, which are, for historical reasons, also known as creative sets. Goedel's insight that provable theorems in (sufficiently rich) axiomatized theories form creative sets and that the true theorems for rich mathematical systems form productive sets [38] showed that it is impossible to axiomatize consistently such fields as number theory and set theory and has to be considered one of the most far reaching achievements in logic.

We recall that all complete r.e. sets are recursively isomorphic [38].

FACT. *If A, $A \subseteq \Sigma^*$, and B, $B \subseteq \Gamma^*$, are complete r.e. sets then there exists a recursive bijection ρ such that*

$$w \in A \iff \rho(w) \in B.$$

In the early 1970s it was discovered that some natural (resource bounded) recursive families of languages had complete languages under polynomial time reductions. For example, it was discovered that the family of languages accepted by nondeterministic Turing machines in polynomial time, *NP*, contains complete problems under polynomial time reductions, that the family *NP* contains many problems of practical importance and that many of these problems are complete in *NP* [1], [11], [31]. It was also discovered that the family of languages accepted by Turing machines on polynomial tape, *PTAPE*, possessed many natural complete problems under polynomial time reductions [1], [31].

Since the early 1970s the study of different families of languages defined in terms of their computational complexity, referred to as the study of the structure of feasible computations, has revealed a handful of further families of languages which have intuitively natural definitions and which possess a wide variety of natural problems which are complete for the respective classes under resource bounded reductions [1], [10], [12], [24], [28]–[30], [41], [43]. At the present this is one of the very active research areas in computational complexity which has unified a number of results and revealed some unexpected connections as well as focused our attention on a set of important open problems [1], [11], [25], [41].

In this chapter we give the necessary background information, define resource bounded reductions, and define and discuss the most prominent natural classes of computations and complete problems for these classes.

As stated before, we let

$$M_1, M_2, M_3, \ldots$$

be a standard enumeration of Turing machines and denote by

$$L(M_i)$$

the set accepted by machine M_i. Let

$$T_i(n) = \max\{\text{number of steps performed by } M_i \text{ on input } w \mid w \in \Sigma^n\}$$

$$L_i(n) = \max\{\text{number of tape squares used by } M_i \text{ on input } w \mid w \in \Sigma^n\}.$$

Let

$$TIME[T(n)] = \{L(M_i) \mid T_i(n) \leqq T(n)\}$$

and

$$TAPE[T(n)] = \{L(M_i) \mid L_i(n) \leqq T(n)\}.$$

In order to permit us to study computations which require less than linear amount of tape in the length of the input we separate the working tape from the input and output tape.

DEFINITION. A log *n-tape transducer* or an L-*transducer* is a deterministic three tape Tm with a two-way read-only input tape, a one-way write-only output tape and (for input of length n) a $\log n$ long two-way, read-write work tape. We say that a function is log *n-tape* or L-*computable* if it can be computed by an L-transducer.

DEFINITION. A set A, $A \subseteq \Sigma^*$, is *reduced* to a set B, $B \subseteq \Gamma^*$, by the function f iff

$$x \in A \quad \Leftrightarrow \quad f(x) \in B.$$

A set is A log n-*tape reducible* or L-*reducible* to a set B if A is reducible to B by an L-computable function; we shall write

$$A \leqq_{\mathrm{L}} B.$$

A set A is p-*reducible* to B if A is reducible to B by a function computable in polynomial time on a Tm.

Let G be a family of languages.

DEFINITION. A, $A \subseteq \Sigma^*$, is L-*complete* or *complete* for G if

1. $A \in G$
2. $(\forall B \in G)\,[B \leqq_{\mathrm{L}} A]$.

Thus, in a strong technical sense, a complete language in a family of languages is one to which we can easily (on log n-tape) reduce the recognition problem of any other language in the family.

It is interesting to recall that the original definition of complete sets for the classic family of languages *NP*, the family of languages accepted by nondeterministic Tm's in polynomial time, was given in terms of reductions defined by polynomial time computations of Tm's with the complete set as an oracle set; this corresponds to the concept of Turing reducibility in recursive function theory [11], [38]. Soon after that it was realized that all specific reductions used in this study can be performed by polynomial time bounded Tm's, as defined above, corresponding to many-one reducibility in recursive-function theory [31], [38]. Since then it has been observed that all the known reductions of sets in *NP* to complete sets in *NP* can actually be carried out on log n-tape transducers [28], [42]. As a matter of fact, all other known p-time reductions to complete sets in *PTAPE*, *EXPTAPE*, etc. are also log n-tape reductions, and the previously stated completeness results can all be restated in terms of L-reductions. In view of this observation we will formulate and state all our reductions and completeness results in terms of L-reductions and L-isomorphisms. Furthermore, the use of L-reductions will permit us to extend uniformly our results to classes which are apparently computationally simpler than *NP*, for which polynomial time reductions are computationally too powerful [21], [28]–[30].

We now define and discuss the best known natural families of languages determined by computational complexity bounds.

$$L = TAPE[\log n] = \{L(M_i) \mid L_i(n) \leqq \log n\}$$

$$NL = NDTAPE[\log n] = \{L(M_i) \mid M_i \text{ nondet. and } L_i(n) \leqq \log n\}$$

$$DCSL = TAPE[n] = \{L(M_i) \mid L_i(n) \leqq n\}$$

$$CSL = NDTAPE[n] = \{L(M_i) \mid M_i \text{ nondet. and } L_i(n) \leqq n\}$$

$$P = \{L(M_i) \mid T_i(n) \leqq n^k,\ k = 1, 2, 3, \ldots\}$$

$$NP = \{L(M_i) | M_i \text{ nondet. and } T_i(n) \leqq n^k, k = 1, 2, 3, \ldots\}$$

$$PTAPE = \{L(M_i) | L_i(n) \leqq n^k, k = 1, 2, 3, \ldots\}$$

$$EXPTIME = \{L(M_i) | T_i(n) \leqq 2^{cn}, c > 0\}$$

$$EXPTAPE = \{L(M_i) | L_i(n) \leqq 2^{cn}, c > 0\}.$$

The class L consists of all languages which can be accepted on $\log n$-tape. Since on $\log n$-tape we can count up to a polynomial of n where the polynomial depends on the size of the working tape alphabet, we see that L consists of all the languages which can be accepted by algorithms which can count up to a polynomial in the length of the family L in terms of finite multi-head automata [24].

Consider finite automata (f.a.) with one input tape on which we place the input bounded by special end markers; the automaton has k, $k = 1, 2, \ldots$, two-way, read-only heads which cannot go past the two end markers enclosing the input string. The automaton is started by placing all k heads on the first input symbol and the automaton accepts by entering an accepting final state. Let $F_1, F_2, \ldots$ be a standard enumeration of such finite, multi-head automata.

THEOREM 2.1. *$L = TAPE[\log n] = \{L(F_i) | F_i$ multi-head f.a.$\}$.*

Proof. Use a straightforward simulation argument [24]. □

For other characterizations of L in terms of elementary flow charts see [24].

The class NL, correspondingly, consists of the languages which can be accepted by non-deterministic Tm's which can count up to a polynomial in n. Furthermore, NL can also be characterized in terms of nondeterministic multihead finite automata.

THEOREM 2.2. *$NL = \{L(F_i) | F_i$ nondet. multi-head f.a.$\}$.*

Proof. The proof is similar to the previous one. □

It is not known whether

$$L \subsetneqq NL.$$

The best containment relation is given by [1], [39]:

$$TAPE[\log n] = L \subseteqq NL \subseteqq TAPE[\log^2 n].$$

The classes $DCSL$ and CSL consist of the deterministic and nondeterministic context-sensitive languages, and are well known [24], [27]. Again, it is not known whether

$$DCSL \subsetneqq CSL,$$

and the best containment result is given by [1], [39]:

$$TAPE[n] = DCSL \subseteqq CSL \subseteqq TAPE[n^2].$$

It is also known that [24], [39]

$$L = NL \quad \Rightarrow \quad DCSL = CSL.$$

For further discussion of these problems see [24].

The family P, consisting of all the languages which can be accepted by deterministic Tm's in polynomial time, is considered as the fundamental family of *feasible* computations.

At the same time, it turns out that the family NP, consisting of nondeterministic Tm polynomial time computations, contains many important practical problems. As a matter of fact, the family NP can also be characterized as the set of problems for which we can check in polynomial time whether a proposed solution is an actual solution of our problem. It is easily seen—and we will illustrate it later—that there are very many natural problems of this type. At the present it is not known whether

$$P \subsetneqq NP,$$

and this has to be considered as the major open problem about feasible computations [1], [25].

Intuitively, the $P = NP$? problem is the fundamental problem whether guessing in problem solving can be systematically eliminated without the need of exhausting in essence all possible guesses. If this is not possible then

$$P \neq NP$$

and, the complete problems in NP cannot be computed in polynomial time, which shows that many problems of practical importance are not feasibly computable.

The family $PTAPE$, consisting of all the languages accepted on polynomial tape, contains many interesting problems from logic, combinatorics and game theory [1], [25], [31], [40]. It is known [39] that

$$PTAPE = NDPTAPE$$

and that

$$L \subseteq NL \subsetneqq PTAPE.$$

On the other hand, it is not known whether

$$P \subsetneqq PTAPE \quad \text{or} \quad NP \subsetneqq PTAPE.$$

It is strongly conjectured that

$$P \neq NP \neq PTAPE,$$

but so far, all attempts to resolve this problem have failed.

Finally, the families $EXPTIME$ and $EXPTAPE$ also contain some interesting complete problems showing that they are definitely not feasibly computable. It is known that

$$P \subseteq NP \subseteq PTAPE \subseteq EXPTIME \subseteq EXPTAPE,$$

but it is not known whether any of these containments are proper, except for $P \subsetneqq EXPTIME$ and $PTAPE \subsetneqq EXPTAPE$.

Again, if

$$P = PTAPE$$

then it follows that

$$EXPTIME = EXPTAPE,$$

but the possibility is still open that

$$PTIME \subsetneqq PTAPE \quad \text{and} \quad EXPTIME = EXPTAPE.$$

From the above summary it is clearly seen that computational complexity theory faces some fundamental unsolved problems about the containment relations between the families of languages

$$N, \ NL, \ DSCL, \ CSL, \ P, \ NP, \ PTAPE, \ EXPTIME \ \text{and} \ EXPTAPE.$$

We conjecture that all these families of languages are different and that we will have to find new proof techniques to show this fact. So far the separation proofs, for the cases we know to be different, have been all based on straightforward diagonalization between classes with the same resource bound or simulation, such as

$$L \text{ and } PTAPE \quad \text{or} \quad P \text{ and } EXPTIME$$

and the use of the result that

$$NDTAPE(L_i(n)) \subseteq TAPE(L_i(n)^2),$$

which yields, for example, that

$$NL \subseteq PTAPE.$$

Later in this chapter we will show that

$$DCSL \neq P,$$

but it is not known whether

$$DCSL \subseteq P \quad \text{or} \quad P \subseteq DCSL$$

or neither condition holds.

At the same time, these families of languages have interesting complete sets and they have served a very useful role in classifying problems according to their computational complexity. For example, showing that the problem of determining whether a game (from a given family of games) has a winning strategy is complete in *PTAPE* is very strong evidence (though not yet a proof) that the determination of winning strategies for this family of games is not a feasible computation [13], [40]. Clearly, showing that a certain word problem in algebra is complete for *EXPTAPE* is proof that this word problem is not feasibly computable [12].

As a matter of fact, one of the considerable achievements of computational complexity theory is to have shown that many innocuous looking computable problems in algebra, logic, theory of computation and combinatorics are not practically solvable [1], [10], [12], [14], [41], [42].

Next we prove in a uniform way the existence of complete sets for all previously defined families of languages. We will do this by just observing that the universal languages for these families form complete sets, just as the set

$$\{(M_i, x) | x \in L(M_i)\}$$

was complete for the family of r.e. sets. As in the case of r.e. complete sets, the natural complete sets are far more interesting than the universal sets, but the universal sets very easily show the existence of complete sets. We will discuss natural complete sets later.

THEOREM 2.3. *The families NL, DCSC, CSL, P, NP, PTAPE, EXPTIME and EXPTAPE have L-complete sets.*

Proof. Since all the proofs that the universal sets are complete for the corresponding families of languages are similar, we will only prove it, as an illustration, for *NL* and *P*.

For the sake of simplicity we assume that $M_1, M_2, \ldots$ have a fixed input alphabet Σ and let $\#$ be a new symbol, $\# \notin \Sigma$ nor is $\#$ used in the description of M_i. Let

$$U_{NL} = \{M_i \; \# \; x \; \# \; (\#^{|x||M_i|}) | \text{nondet. } M_i \text{ accepts } x \text{ on } \log |x| \text{ tape}\}.$$

It is seen that U_{NL} is in *NL*, since a fixed nondeterministic Tm, M_u, can accept U_{NL} on $\log n$-tape; M_u has enough tape to encode the possibly larger tape alphabet of M_i, and simulate M_i on input x (since $L_i(n) \leqq \log n$) on tape

$$|M_i| \log |x| \leqq \log [|M_i \; \# \; x \; \# \; (\#^{|x||M_i|})|].$$

Furthermore, the mapping σ_i

$$x \mapsto M_i \; \# \; x \; \# \; (\#^{|x||M_i|})$$

is such that, for any nondeterministic M_i with $L_i(n) \leqq \log n$, we have

$$x \in L(M_i) \quad \text{iff} \quad \sigma_i(x) \in U_{NL}$$

and, it is easily seen that σ_i is computable on $\log n$-tape. Thus U_{NL} is L-complete for the family *NL*.

To obtain a complete language for *P* let $M_{i,k}$ be a Tm such that

$$T_{i,k}(n) \leqq n^k$$

and

$$M_{i,k}(x) = \textbf{if } T_i(|x|) \leqq |x|^k \textbf{ then } M_i(x) \textbf{ else } \text{reject}.$$

Clearly, $M_{i,k}$ can be easily obtained from M_i by attaching on a separate set of tapes an n^k counter.

Thus we see that

$$P = \{L(M_{i,k}) | i, k = 1, 2, 3, \ldots\}.$$

A complete (universal) language for P is given by

$$U_P = \{M_{i,k} \ \# \ x \ \# \ (\#^{|M_{i,k}|\,|x|^k}) | x \in L(M_{i,k}),\ i,\ k = 1, 2, 3, \ldots\}.$$

Again it is easily seen that U_P is in P and that $L(M_{i,k})$ is L-reducible to U_P by the mapping

$$x \mapsto M_{i,k} \ \# \ x \ \# \ (\#^{|M_{i,k}|\,|x|^k}).$$

Thus U_P is an L-complete language for P.

The corresponding complete languages for the other families of languages are constructed similarly to the ones for NL and P. This establishes the existence of complete sets for the families of languages listed in the theorem. □

We now list some natural complete languages for the above mentioned families of languages. Though there have been discovered a bewildering number of (hundreds of) complete problems for such families as NP, we will only list a few to give the reader a feel for how the nature of the complete problems change as we move up through the families NL, CSL, P, NP and $PTAPE$. The discovery of the richness and apparent diversity of natural complete problems for most of these families of languages has been one of the surprising developments during the mid-1970s, and it testifies to the naturalness of these families of languages and their role in classifying problems according to their computational complexity.

We first list some problems complete for NL [30].

The graph accessibility problem, GAP:

INPUT: A directed graph G with an "in" and "out" node.

PROPERTY: G has a directed path from "in" to "out" node.

The unsatisfiability problem, UNSAT:

INPUT: A Boolean formula F in conjunctive normal form with no more than two literals per clause.

PROPERTY: F is not satisfiable, i.e., $F \neq 1$ for all assignments of the variables.

The associative generation problem, AGEN:

INPUT: A finite set A, an associative binary operation $\circ$ defined in A, a subset S of A and an element $w \in A$.

PROPERTY: w is generated by elements in S.

The following problems are complete for P [29].

Context-free language emptiness problem, CFL$\varnothing$:

INPUT: Context-free grammar G,

PROPERTY: $L(G) = \varnothing$.

Context-free language infinity problem, CFL∞:

INPUT: Context-free grammar G.

PROPERTY: $|L(G)| = \infty$.

The generation problem, GEN:

INPUT: A finite set A, binary operation $\cdot$ on A, a subset S, $S \subseteq A$, and an element w of A.

PROPERTY: w is generated by elements in S.

The following problems are complete for *NP* [11], [24], [31], [34].

The conjunctive normal form Boolean satisfiability problem, CNF–SAT:

INPUT: A Boolean formula F in conjunctive normal form (we need no more than three terms per clause).

PROPERTY: There exists an assignment of "zeros" and "ones" to the variables of F such that $F = 1$.

The Hamiltonian circuit problem, HAM:

INPUT: A graph G.

PROPERTY: G has a simple cycle which goes through all vertices.

The regular expression problem, REG:

INPUT: Two regular expression R_i and R_j over $\Sigma, \cdot, \cup,), ($.

PROPERTY: $L(R_i) \neq L(R_j)$.

The Diophantine quadratic equation problem, DIOPH:

INPUT: An equation $az^2 + by - c = 0$ with positive integer coefficients.

PROPERTY: The equation $ax^2 + by - c = 0$ has a positive integer solution.

The following problems are complete for *PTAPE* [1], [13], [40]–[42].

The quantified Boolean formula satisfiability problem, QSAT:

INPUT: A quantified Boolean formula in conjunctive normal form, for example,

$$(\forall x_1, x_2)(\exists x_3)(\forall x_4, x_5)F(x_1, x_2, \ldots, x_5) = QF.$$

PROPERTY: QF is satisfiable.

The game *HEX* is played by two players on a graph G with two distinguished nodes "in" and "out", Player I places blue markers on unmarked nodes (except "in" and "out") and Player II places red markers on unmarked nodes. Player I starts and they alternate placing one marker on each move. Player I wins if he has a blue sequence of nodes leading from "in" to "out" node.

The winning strategy problem, HEX:

INPUT: A graph G with an "in" and "out" node.

PROPERTY: The first player has a winning strategy for (G, "in", "out").

The function generation problem, FGEN:

INPUT: A finite set A and a set of functions F mapping A into A, and a function $f: A \to A$.

PROPERTY: The function f can be expressed as a composition of functions in F.

*The regular expression problem with *, REG**:

INPUT: A regular expression R over $\Sigma, \cdot, \cup, *,), ($.

PROPERTY: $L(R) \neq \Sigma^*$.

The problems *REG** and *FGEN* which are complete for *PTAPE* are also complete for the family of context-sensitive languages, *CSL*.

We have listed only a few representative complete problems for the classes

NL, *P*, *NP*, *PTAPE* and *CSL*.

There are many more complete problems known for these classes; in particular the number of known complete problems for *NP* is very large and still growing.

On the other hand, already from our small list we can learn how the type of problem changes as we move up through our classes. For example, the generation problems *AGEN*, *GEN* and *FGEN* are complete for *NL*, *P* and *PTAPE*. The regular expression problems *REG* and *REG** are, respectively, complete for *NP* and *PTAPE*.

It is interesting to recall that the regular expression problem becomes computationally terribly complex if we permit the use of complement, ¬, in our formulas. It has been shown [41] that the set

$$\{R \mid R \text{ reg. expr. over } \Sigma, \cdot, \cup, \neg, {}^*,), (\text{ with } L(R) = \emptyset\}$$

is not in

$$TAPE\left[2^{2^{\cdot^{\cdot^{\cdot^{2^n}}}}}\right\} k \text{ times}\Big]$$

for any fixed k.

We are now in a position to prove, for the sake of completeness that certain families of languages cannot be equal [43].

THEOREM 2.4. *$P \neq DCSL$, $P \neq CSL$, $NP \neq DCSL$ and $NP \neq CSL$.*

Proof. If

$$DCSL = P$$

then for some n^{k_0} the universal complete language for *DCSL*,

$$U_{DCSL} = \{M_i \# x \#^{|x| \cdot |M_i|} \mid M_i \text{ accepts } x \text{ on tape } |x|\},$$

is in $TIME[n^{k_0}]$. Furthermore, for every A in P there is a deterministic linearly bounded automaton (dlba), M_A, such that $A = L(M_A)$ and an L-reduction of A to U_{DCSL},

$$x \mapsto M_A \# x \#^{|x| \cdot |M_A|}$$

which is computable in time $\leqq C_A \cdot |x|$ for some $C_A > 0$. But then

$$P \subseteq TIME[n^{k_0}],$$

which is a contradiction to the fact that [22], [27]

$$TIME[n^{k_0}] \subsetneqq TIME[n^{k_0+1}].$$

The other cases follow by a very similar argument. □

CHAPTER 3

L-Isomorphisms of Complete Sets

In the previous section we saw that the families of languages

$$NL, \quad CSL, \quad P, \quad NP \quad \text{and} \quad PTAPE$$

have complete problems and that many natural problems form complete problems for these families. In this section we will show that all the known complete sets for these families are, respectively, similar in a very strong technical sense. More precisely, we will show that all the known complete sets for the different classes are, respectively, L-isomorphic. This result implies that all the previously "known" complete sets in *NP*, *PTAPE*, etc. are p-isomorphic as was shown in [3], [4] and extends in a uniform way the L-isomorphism results to where the p-isomorphism results did not apply [21].

Recall that all the r.e. complete sets are isomorphic under recursive mappings. A proof, for example, that all complete sets in *NL* are L-isomorphic would imply that

$$L \subsetneqq NL,$$

and would solve a classic open problem [4], [21]. We summarize such results below.

THEOREM 3.1. *If all L-complete sets in NL are L-isomorphic then*

$$L \subsetneqq NL.$$

If all L-complete sets in P and NL are, respectively, L-isomorphic then

$$L \subsetneqq P \quad \text{and} \quad L \subsetneqq NP.$$

Proof. If $L = P$ then any set in P can be recognized by a log n-tape Tm and therefore there exist finite sets which are L-complete for P. On the other hand, if all L-complete sets of P are isomorphic then they all must be infinite. Thus isomorphism of these sets implies that $L \neq P$. The other cases follow by similar arguments. □

We now start our investigation of L-isomorphisms with the goal of developing very simple necessary and sufficient conditions that a new complete set in one of the previously listed families of languages is L-isomorphic to the previously known complete sets in that family, thus showing that in a very strong technical sense all the "known" complete sets in these families of languages are indeed very similar.

THEOREM 3.2. *Let p and q be L-reductions of A to B and B to A, $A \subseteq \Sigma^*$, $B \subseteq \Gamma^*$, respectively, such that*

a) *p and q are one-to-one,*

b) p^{-1} *and* q^{-1} *are L-computable,*
c) $|p(z)|>|z|^2$ *and* $|q(z)|>|z|^2$.
Then A and B are L-isomorphic.

Proof. From p and q we will construct an isomorphism ϕ between A and B and show that ϕ and ϕ^{-1} are L-computable.

Let

$$R_1=\{(q\circ p)^k x \mid k\geqq 0 \text{ and } x\notin q(\Gamma^*)\},$$
$$R_2=\{q\circ(p\circ q)^k x \mid k\geqq 0 \text{ and } x\notin p(\Sigma^*)\},$$
$$S_1=\{(p\circ q)^k x \mid k\geqq 0 \text{ and } x\notin p(\Sigma^*)\},$$
$$S_2=\{p\circ(q\circ p)^k x \mid k\geqq 0 \text{ and } x\notin q(\Gamma^*)\}.$$

It is easily seen that

$$R_1\cap R_2=S_1\cap S_2=\varnothing, \quad \text{and} \quad \Sigma^*=R_1\cup R_2, \quad \Gamma^*=S_1\cup S_2.$$

Assume that if $p^{-1}(z)$ or $q^{-1}(z)$ are undefined then they can output a special symbol *, since we can detect cycling on log n-tape.

Define

$$\phi(z)=\textbf{if } z\in R_1 \textbf{ then } p(z) \textbf{ else } q^{-1}(z)$$
$$\phi^{-1}(z)=\textbf{if } z\in S_2 \textbf{ then } p^{-1}(z) \textbf{ else } q(z).$$

We first show that ϕ and ϕ^{-1} have the desired properties and then show that ϕ and ϕ^{-1} are L-computable. Since

$$R_1\cap R_2=\varnothing \quad \text{and} \quad R_1\cup R_2=\Sigma^*$$

the function ϕ is well defined. Similarly $\phi^{-1}(z)$ is well defined. It is seen that

$$\phi(R_1)=S_2, \quad \phi(R_2)=S_1, \quad \phi^{-1}(S_2)=R_1, \quad \phi^{-1}(S_1)=R_2,$$

and that ϕ is a one-to-one onto mapping and that ϕ and ϕ^{-1} are indeed inverses. To see that ϕ is a reduction of A to B recall that

$$z\in A \quad \text{iff} \quad p(z)\in B \quad \text{and} \quad x\in B \quad \text{iff} \quad q(x)\in A.$$

Since

$$\phi(z)=\textbf{if } z\in R_1 \textbf{ then } p(z) \textbf{ else } q^{-1}(z)$$

we conclude that

$$z\in A \quad \text{iff} \quad \phi(z)\in B.$$

To compute $\phi(z)$ we have to determine whether z is in R_1 or R_2. This can be done by computing the minimal $k\geqq 0$ such that

$$(q^{-1}\circ p^{-1}\circ)^k q^{-1}(z)=* \quad \text{or} \quad p^{-1}\circ(q^{-1}\circ p^{-1}\circ)^k q^{-1}(z)=*.$$

In the first case

$$\phi(z)=p(z);$$

in the second case

$$\phi(z)=q^{-1}(z).$$

Since p and q are such that

$$|p(z)|>|z|^2 \quad \text{and} \quad |q(z)|>|z|^2,$$

we see that

$$|p^{-1}(z)|<|z|^{1/2} \quad \text{and} \quad |q^{-1}(z)|<|z|^{1/2}.$$

Since

$$\log|z|^{1/2}=\tfrac{1}{2}\log|z|$$

we see that the tape requirements for computations of successive inverses are cut in half. This fact can be exploited to compute $\phi(z)$ and $\phi^{-1}(z)$ on log n-tape. The only difficulty is that during the computation there may be intermediate values for

$$q^{-1}(z), \quad p^{-1}\circ q^{-1}(z), \quad q^{-1}\circ p^{-1}\circ q^{-1}(z), \quad \text{etc.}$$

which are too large to be written down on the available working tape. This difficulty can be avoided by never writing these values down but recomputing them (recursively) when they are required in the subsequent computations.

We now outline how this computation is performed on Tm M_ϕ. We can assume that the Tm's computing p and q use exactly $\log|w|$-tape for input w and let M_ϕ have effectively $8\log|w|$-tape available for input w (this can be achieved by choosing a sufficiently large tape alphabet). Let the tape of M_ϕ be divided in $\log|w|$ segments of length

$$4\log|w|, \quad 2\log|w|, \quad \log|w|, \quad \tfrac{1}{2}\log|w|, \quad \text{etc.}$$

These segments will be used to compute, respectively,

$$q^{-1}(w), \quad p^{-1}\circ q^{-1}(w), \quad q^{-1}\circ p^{-1}\circ q^{-1}(w), \quad \text{etc.,}$$

as far as needed to determine whether

$$\phi(w)=p(w) \quad \text{or} \quad \phi(w)=q^{-1}(w).$$

We will refer to the computations of

$$q^{-1}(w), \quad p^{-1}\circ q^{-1}(w), \ldots,$$

respectively, as the first stage, second stage, etc. On each tape segment for each stage of the computation will be recorded the state of the Tm (which computes p^{-1} or q^{-1} of the output of the previous stage), the contents of the work tape of this Tm and which tape square it is scanning; furthermore it will be recorded which tape symbol it is scanning on the (simulated) input tape and how many output symbols it has received from the previous stage.

The computation starts by the first stage computing the first output symbol of $q^{-1}(w)$.

If during the computation in a given stage an output symbol is computed, the computation in this stage stops and the output symbol is passed to the next stage which becomes active. If this output symbol permits the next stage to continue its computation, it computes until it produces an output or needs a new input. In the first case the next stage is activated and the output is passed on; in the second case, the previous stage is activated and an output is requested. In this manner all stages are cycling through computing (many times over) their output which is passed on to the next stage for it to find the appropriate input symbol it is waiting for. At some point one of the computations must yield a * from which M_ϕ can determine whether to compute $p(w)$ or $q^{-1}(w)$ to get $\phi(w)$, which again can be done on $\log |w|$-tape.

This completes the proof that there exists an L-isomorphism between the sets A and B. □

Next we derive several technical results which will lead to a very simple test giving necessary and sufficient conditions that a complete set is L-isomorphic to a fixed, well known complete set in the class under consideration.

First, we derive a condition under which a $\log n$-tape reduction can yield a one-to-one $\log n$-tape invertible reduction.

LEMMA 3.3. *Let A be a set for which two L-computable functions $S_A(\ ,\ )$ and $D_A(\ )$ exist such that*

1) $(\forall x, y)[S_A(x, y) \in A \text{ iff } x \in A]$

2) $(\forall x, y)[D_A(S(x, y)) = y]$.

Then if f is any L-reduction of C to A, the map

$$f'(x) = S_A[f(x), x]$$

is a one-to-one L-reduction of C to A and $(f')^{-1}$ is L-computable.

Proof. From condition 1) we see that

$$S_A[f(x), x]$$

is an L-reduction of C to A since

$$x \in C \quad \text{iff} \quad f(x) \in A \quad \text{iff} \quad S_A[f(x), x] \in A.$$

To see that f' is one-to-one assume that

$$f'(x) = f'(y);$$

then

$$x = D_A[f'(x)] = D_A[S_A(f(x), x)] = D_A[S_A(f(y), y)] = D_A[f'(y)] = y$$

so f' is a one-to-one map. Furthermore,

$$q(x) = \textbf{if } x = S_A[f(D_A(x)), D_A(x)] \textbf{ then } D_A(x) \textbf{ else}^*$$

is the inverse of f' and since S_A, D_A and f are all $\log n$-tape computable so is $(f')^{-1}$, as was to be shown. □

To apply Theorem 3.2 we still need the length squaring property, which we consider next.

Let $A \subseteq \Sigma^*$. Then $Z_A: \Sigma^* \to \Sigma^*$ is a *padding function* for the set A if

1. $Z_A(x) \in A$ iff $x \in A$
2. Z_A is one-to-one.

LEMMA 3.4. *Let f be a one-to-one L-reduction of A to B and let f^{-1} be L-computable. Assume that either A or B has a padding function Z_X ($X = A$ or B) which satisfies the conditions*:

1) *Z_X and Z_X^{-1} are L-computable,*
2) $(\forall y)\,[|Z_X(y)| > |y|^2 + 1]$.

Then there exists a one-to-one L-reduction f' of A to B such that

i) *$(f')^{-1}$ is L-computable,*
ii) $(\forall y)\,[|f'(y)| > |y|^2]$.

Proof. Let $X = A$. Since f and f^{-1} are L-computable there exists a (nondecreasing) polynomial p such that $p(n) > n^2$ and

$$\forall(x)[|f(x)| < p(|x|) \quad \text{and} \quad |f^{-1}(x)| < p(|x|)].$$

Then from condition 2) we know that there exists an integer r such that

$$(\forall x)[|Z_A^r(x)| > p(|x|^2)].$$

Therefore

$$|f \circ Z_A^r(x)| > |x|^2,$$

since

$$|f \circ Z_A^r(x)| \leqq |x|^2$$

implies that

$$|f^{-1} \circ f \circ Z_A^r(x)| = |Z_A^r(x)| \leqq p(|x|^2),$$

which is a contradiction. Thus

$$f'(x) = f \circ Z_A^r(x)$$

is an L-reduction of A to B with the desired properties.

Assume that the padding function, Z_B, exists for the set B. Then there exists an integer r such that for all x

$$|Z_B^r(x)| > p \circ p(|x|)$$

where p is the polynomial defined in the first part of the proof. Then

$$(\forall x)[p(|f(x)|) \geqq |x|],$$

since

$$p(|f(x)|) < |x|$$

implies that $f(x) = y$ and

$$|f^{-1}(y)| < p(|y|) < |x|,$$

which contradicts the fact that

$$f^{-1} \circ f(x) = x.$$

But then

$$f' = Z_B^r \circ f$$

is a one-to-one L-reduction of A to B with $(f')^{-1}$ L-computable, and

$$|f'(x)| = |Z_B^r \circ f(x)| > p \circ p(|f(x)|) \geqq p(|x|) > |x|^2.$$

This completes the proof. □

We now combine these results to get our next result.

THEOREM 3.5. *Let the set A be L-reducible to B and B be L-reducible to A; furthermore let the set A have a padding function Z_A satisfying Lemma* 3.4 *and function S_A and D_A satisfying Lemma* 3.3. *Then B is L-isomorphic to A iff B has functions S_B and D_B satisfying Lemma* 3.3.

Proof. If A and B are L-isomorphic under the bijection ϕ then we can define

$$S_B[x, y] = \phi^{-1} \circ S_A[\phi(x), y]$$

and

$$D_B(x) = D_A[\phi(x)].$$

(Note that we can always choose S_A such that $S_A: \Sigma^* \times \{0, 1\}^* \to \Sigma^*$ and $S_B: \Gamma^* \times \{0, 1\}^* \to \Gamma^*$, which we have done in this construction.) Clearly, S_B and D_B are L-computable since S_A, D_A, ϕ and ϕ^{-1} are. Furthermore for all x and y

$$x \in B \quad \text{iff} \quad \phi(x) \in A \quad \text{iff} \quad S_A[\phi(x), y] \in A$$
$$\text{iff} \quad \phi^{-1} \circ S_A[\phi(x), y] = S_B[x, y] \in B$$

and

$$D_B[S_B(x, y)] = y.$$

Conversely, if the functions S_B and D_B exist then by using Lemmas 3.3 and 3.4 with Theorem 3.2 we get an L-isomorphism between A and B. This completes the proof. □

To apply the previously developed result, Theorem 3.5, we will pick from each of the families *NL*, *CSL*, *P*, *NP* and *PTAPE* the universal complete language and show that each of these languages has a padding function Z_A and functions D_A and S_A satisfying Lemmas 3.3 and 3.4, respectively. Then any complete set B in the corresponding class will be L-isomorphic to these "classic" sets if and only if B possesses the two L-computable functions S_B and D_B, satisfying Lemma 3.3. As it will be seen from examples, this is a very simple test.

LEMMA 3.6. *The universal complete languages for NL, DCSL, CSL, P, NP, PTAPE and EXPTAPE have the padding function Z_u and functions D_u and S_u satisfying Lemmas* 3.3 *and* 3.4, *respectively.*

Proof. We give a proof for the family *NP*. Recall that

$$U_{NP}=\{M_{i,k}\ \#\ x\ \#\ (\#^{|x|^k\cdot|M_{i,k}|})|M_{i,k} \text{ nondet. and accepts } x \text{ in time } |x|^k\}.$$

The padding function Z_u maps

$$M_{i,k}\ \#\ x\ \#\ (\#^{|x|^k\cdot|M_{i,k}|})\mapsto M'_{i,k}\ \#\ x\ \#\ (\#^{|x|^k\cdot|M'_{i,k}|})$$

where $M'_{i,k}$ is $M_{i,k}$ with sufficiently many new states added (which are inaccessible from the starting state) to insure that

$$|Z_u(w)|>|w|^2.$$

Clearly Z_u is L-computable and

$$w\in U_{NP} \quad \text{iff} \quad Z_u(w)\in U_{NP}.$$

Similarly, the function S_u maps

$$(M_{i,k}\ \#\ x\ \#\ (\#^{|x|^k\cdot|M_{i,k}|}),\ y)\mapsto M_{i,k}^{(y)}\ \#\ x\ \#\ (\#^{|x|^k\cdot|M_{i,k}^{(y)}|})$$

(if the input format is not correct, then $(z, y)\mapsto \#\ z\ \#\ y$), where $M_{i,k}^{(y)}$ is obtained from $M_{i,k}$ by adding new states, not accessible from the old states, to encode the string

$$y=y_1y_2\ldots y_j\in\{0, 1\}^*.$$

The new states are added at the end of the description of $M_{i,k}$ as follows: first two new states with transitions between them are added (as a marker so that D_u can detect where the encoding starts), these states are followed by a sequence of states, one state for each symbol of y, where the ith state has no transitions if $y_i=0$ and a transition back to itself if $y_i=1$. It is easily seen that D_u and S_u are L-computable, that

$$S_u(w, y)\in U_{NP} \quad \text{iff} \quad w\in U_{NP}$$

and

$$D_u\circ S_u(w, y)=y.$$

The proofs for the other families are similar to the above proof. □

We now can derive our necessary and sufficient conditions that a complete set is L-isomorphic to one of the universal complete sets for the respective family of languages.

THEOREM 3.7. *Any L-complete set B in NL, DCSL, CSL, P, NP, PTAPE, EXPTIME or EXPTAPE is, respectively, L-isomorphic to the corresponding universal complete set iff there exist two L-computable functions $D_B(\ ,\ )$ and $S_B(\ )$ such that*

1) $(\forall x, y)[D_B(x, y)\in B \Leftrightarrow x\in B]$
2) $(\forall x, y)[S_B\circ D_B(x, y)=y]$.

Proof. The theorem follows from Lemma 3.6 and Theorem 3.5. □

To show how easy these necessary and sufficient conditions are to check we give a few illustrative proofs.

COROLLARY 3.8. *Each of the sets GAP, REG*, CFL∅ and SAT are, respectively, L-isomorphic to the universal sets in NL, CSL or PTAPE, P and NP.*

Proof. We note that the *GAP* property cannot be destroyed nor introduced by adding a set of new nodes which do not connect to any of the old nodes. We now describe informally the desired functions:

1. $S_{GAP}(x, y)$ (let $x \in \Sigma^*$ and $y \in \{0, 1\}^*$) adds to the graph described by x a new node with two edges looping back to itself and then encodes y in a sequence of new nodes with one edge or no-edge, representing ones and zeros, respectively.
2. D_{GAP} is such that

$$D_{GAP} \circ S_{GAP}(x, y) = y.$$

It is easily seen that all these functions are L-computable and therefore by Theorem 3.7 *GAP* is L-isomorphic to the universal language.

Next we consider the set *REG**, which is complete for *CSL* and *PTAPE*. We denote the corresponding functions by D_R and S_R.

1. $S_R(R, y) = y + (\Lambda + 0 + 1)^{|y|} + (0+1)^{|y|+1} R$
2. $D_R \circ S_R(R, y) = y$.

Again it is easily seen that the functions have the desired properties and that D_R and S_R are L-computable.

For the *CFL∅* problem let the context-free grammar be given by

$$G = (N, T, \tau, Pr).$$

where N, T, τ and Pr denote, respectively, the set of nonterminal symbols, the set of terminal symbols, the starting symbol and the set of productions. To construct the desired functions D_c and S_c we will add three new symbols to N and new productions in these symbols (the productions may be repeated many times in Pr) to encode y. For $S_c(G, y) = G'$, $y \in \{0, 1\}^*$, S_c encodes the sequence y in G' with new productions using, $N_1 \to N_1N_1$ as a marker and $N_1 \to N_1N_2$ for a "zero" and $N_1 \to N_1N_3$ for a "one". Clearly D_c and S_c are L-computable and satisfy the required conditions.

Finally, we note that the desired functions D_{SAT} and S_{SAT} exist for the satisfiability problem. Let F have the variables $x_1, x_2, \ldots, x_n$ and let

$$S_{SAT}(F, y) = F \cdot (x_{n+1} + \bar{x}_{n+1}) \cdot z_1 \cdot z_2 \cdot z_3 \cdot \ldots \cdot z_{|y|}$$

where

$$y = y_1 y_2 \ldots y_k \quad \text{and} \quad z_i = \textbf{if } y_i = 0 \textbf{ then } x_{n+i+1} \textbf{ else } \bar{x}_{n+i+1}.$$

Again it is easily seen that this function is L-computable and

$$D_{SAT} \circ S_{SAT}(F, y) = y.$$

This completes the proof. □

As seen from the examples and [3], [4], [5], [21] the necessary and sufficient conditions of Theorem 3.7 are very easy to check. We have checked them for a large number of complete sets for different families of languages without encountering any difficulties. Thus we can assert the following.

CLAIM. *The "known" complete sets for NL, CSL, P, NP, PTAPE, etc. are all, respectively L-isomorphic.*

At the same time it should be recalled that we do not known whether all complete sets in these classes are L-isomorphic. Furthermore, Theorem 3.1 shows that a proof that all complete sets in *NL* or *NP* are, respectively, L-isomorphic would solve some (apparently) hard open problems.

CHAPTER 4

Structure of Complete Sets

In this chapter we investigate further properties of complete sets. We are particularly interested in the denseness of complete sets and the question whether complete sets have easy to recognize subsets [3], [4], [21]. We also show that if $P \neq NP$ then there exist sets in $NP - P$ which are not complete [32].

We first consider the denseness problem.

DEFINITION. A language A, $A \subseteq \Sigma^*$, is *sparse* if there exists a polynomial p such that

$$|A \cap \Sigma^n| \leq p(n).$$

It should be observed that if there would exist a sparse set (recursive or otherwise) to which a complete *NP* problem could be reduced, then the members of this set up to length n could be listed on polynomially long tape, and a Tm equipped with this tape could solve in polynomial time all problems in *NP*. Note that this cannot be done if the set to which we reduce a complete problem in *NP* is not sparse. Thus sparseness corresponds to the possibility of constructing "short" tables which can be effectively used for table look-up to solve problems which are computationally hard.

We will show in the following that the complete sets in *DCSL*, *CSL*, *PTAPE*, *EXPTIME* and *EXPTAPE* cannot be L-reduced to any sparse set. Thus showing that there are no "small amounts of information" which can aid us in their computation.

The problem whether complete sets in *NL*, *P* or *NP* can be L-reduced to sparse sets is still open, and we conjecture that this is not the case. Note that it could happen that all the complete sets of these families are L-isomorphic and therefore not sparse, but that they still can be L-reduced to sparse sets which are harder to compute (or are not even r.e.) than the corresponding complete sets. Again we conjecture that this is not the case.

THEOREM 4.1. *No language L-complete for CSL, PTAPE, EXPTIME or EXPTAPE can be sparse.*

Proof. We will outline a diagonalization process which constructs a nonsparse set A, acceptable on deterministic linear tape, $A \in TAPE[n]$, such that any L-reduction of A to any other set must be one-to-one almost everywhere. Therefore, a complete set to which A is L-reducible cannot be sparse, since one-to-one L-reductions map nonsparse sets into nonsparse sets.

Construction of A. Let $M_1, M_2, \ldots$ be a lexiographically ordered enumeration of all L-transducers and assume that Σ^* is also ordered lexiographically. In the description of the machine M which accepts the set A we will use several auxiliary sets: I_n is a subset of all L-transducers which have been found (processing inputs up to w_n) not to be L-reductions of A to any other set; the set

$$A_n = A \cap \{w \mid w \leqq w_n\}.$$

Let

$$A_1 = \emptyset \quad \text{and} \quad I_1 = \emptyset.$$

For input w_n, $|w_n| \geqq 1$, M lays off $|w_n| = m$ tape squares, and in the subsequent computation this bound is never exceeded. For sake of easy visualization of M we can assume that the different computations described below are performed on separate tracks of the laid off tape.

First, M enumerates (on a track of the available tape) as many L-transducers as possible and marks the ones which are in I_{n-1}. If no unmarked L-transducers are on the list then w_n is accepted, i.e.,

$$A_n = A_{n-1} \cup \{w_n\} \quad \text{and} \quad I_n = I_{n-1}.$$

Otherwise, let $M_{i_1}, M_{i_2}, \ldots, M_{i_s}$ be the unmarked, enumerated L-transducers. M tries successively for $j = 1, 2, \ldots, s$ to find an x, $x < w_n$, such that

$$M_{i_j}(x) = M_{i_j}(w_n).$$

If no x is found w_n is accepted and

$$A_n = A_{n-1} \cup \{w_n\} \quad \text{and} \quad I_n = I_{n-1}.$$

If such an x is found, then M determines whether $x \in A_{n-1}$ or $x \notin A_{n-1}$. (This can be done on the available tape since we can erase all previous computations; even if the recursion proceeds further M just has to record whether it is an odd or even number of steps it is recursing backwards to determine whether w_n should be placed in A or not.) In the first case

$$A_n = A_{n-1} \quad \text{and} \quad I_n = I_{n-1} \cup \{M_{ij}\},$$

and in the second case

$$A_n = A_{n-1} \cup \{w_n\} \quad \text{and} \quad I_n = I_{n-1} \cup \{M_{i_j}\}.$$

It can be seen that A is recognizable on linear tape and since the enumeration of $M_1, M_2, \ldots, M_t$ used by M uses at least t tape squares we see that for inputs up to length t at most t inputs can be rejected and therefore A is dense. Finally, it is seen from the construction of A that any L-reduction which is not one-to-one almost everywhere is not a reduction of A to any set. This completes the proof. □

It remains an interesting open question whether *NL*, *P* or *NP* can have, respectively, L-complete sets which are sparse. We conjecture that this is not the case.

We now turn to the problem of finding easy to compute subsets in complete sets. If all complete sets in, say, *NP* are L-isomorphic then all the computational complexity properties of the complete sets are similar modulo a log n-tape permutation. Thus if a given complete set in *NP* has infinite subsets in *P* or *L* then so do all complete sets for *NP*. At the present, we unfortunately do not know whether every complete set in *NP* must be infinite (and therefore $P \neq NP$), nor, if we assume that $P \neq NP$, do we know that every complete set in *NP* must have infinite, deterministic polynomial time computable subsets. On the other hand, we can prove the last result for *DCSL*, *CSL*, *PTAPE*, *EXPTIME* and *EXPTAPE*.

We will prove that every L-complete language in *DCSL* contains infinite subsets which are $\log n$-tape recognizable. This proof generalizes to the classes *CSL*, *PTAPE*, etc. [3].

Our proof is based on constructing a special language, L_0, in *DCSL* such that any recognizer for L_0 must use linear amount of tape on infinite regular subsets in L_0 and then following the image of this set through reductions to complete sets for *DCSL*.

Methods similar to the one used in the construction of the special set L_0 will be used in the study of r.e. complete sets and several other problems later in this monograph.

Let M_i denote the description of the ith Tm such that $M_i \in \Sigma^*$, $w \in \Sigma^*$, $\# \notin \Sigma$. Then let

$$L_0 = \{M_i \# w \mid [(M_i \text{ rejects } M_i \# w) \text{ or } (M_i \text{ uses at least } |M_i \# w|/|M_i| \text{ tape})]\}.$$

It is easily seen that L_0 is a *DCSL*.

LEMMA 4.2. *If M_0 accepts L_0 then*

1) $\{M_0 \# w \mid w \in \Sigma^*\} \subseteq L_0$

2) *M_0 uses at least $|M_0 \# w|/|M_0|$ tape on input $M_0 \# w$ for all $w \in \Sigma^*$.*

Proof. The machine M_0 cannot use less than $|M_0 \# w|/|M_0|$ tape for the input $M_0 \# w$, since otherwise we can detect on $|M_0 \# w|/|M_0|$ tape whether $M_0 \# w$ is accepted or rejected by M_0, and in either case we get a contradiction that $L_0 = L(M_0)$:

If M_0 accepts $M_0 \# w$ then $M_0 \# w \notin L_0$ by definition of L_0 and vice versa. Thus for every string $M_0 \# w$ the machine M_0 uses at least $|M_0 \# w|/|M_0|$ tape and therefore

$$\{M_0 \# w \mid w \in \Sigma^*\} \subseteq L_0,$$

as was to be shown. □

LEMMA 4.3. *Let H be a complete set of DCSL, let M_H be a deterministic linearly-bounded automaton which accepts H and let f be an L-reduction of L_0 to H. Then $M_0 = M_H \circ f$ is a recognizer of L_0 and there exists a positive integer k_0 such that for almost all w*

$$|f(M_0 \# w)| > |M_0 \# w|^{1/(k_0+1)}.$$

Proof. Since f is an L-transducer there exists an integer $k_0 > 1$ such that

$$(\forall x)\,[|f(x)| < |x|^{k_0}].$$

If

$$|f(M_0 \# w)| < |M_0 \# w|^{1/(k_0+1)}$$

then $M_0 = M_H \circ f$ uses less than

$$\log |M_0 \# w| + |f(M_0 \# w)| < \log |M_0 \# w| + |M_0 \# w|^{1/(k_0+1)}$$

-tape for input $M_0 \# w$, which for large w is less than

$$\frac{|M_0 \# w|}{|M_0|}$$

and thus contradicts Lemma 4.2. Thus for large w

$$|f(M_0 \# w)| > |M_0 \# w|^{1/(k_0+1)}. \quad \square$$

Using the fact, established in the previous lemma, that the L-reduction cannot shrink too much the length of the members from the regular set $\{M_0 \# w | w \in \Sigma^*\}$, we will show that there exists a recognizer for H which uses $\log n$-tape infinitely often.

THEOREM 4.4. *If H is a complete language for DCSL then H has infinite $\log n$-tape recognizable subsets.*

Proof. Let M_H be a dlba which accepts H and let M_0 and f be as defined before. We define a recognizer M'_H for H which will run infinitely often (i.o.) on $\log n$-tape.

Description of M'_H:

1) for input w, M'_H checks for $i = 1$ to $|w|^{(k_0+1)}$ by 1 whether

$$f(M_0 \# 0^i) = w,$$

and accepts if such i is found

2) else simulates M_H on w and accepts iff M_H accepts.

Clearly, M'_H is a dlba. Next we show that $L(M'_H) = H$. By Lemma 4.2

$$\{M_0 \# 0^i | i = 1, 2, \ldots\} \subseteq L(M_0)$$

and therefore

$$\{f(M_0 \# 0^i) | i = 1, 2, \ldots\} \subseteq f[L(M_0)] \subseteq H.$$

Thus w accepted by M_H in part 1) guarantees that $w \in H$. If w is not accepted in part 1) then it is accepted in part 2) iff $w \in L(M_H) = H$. Thus

$$L(M'_H) = H.$$

The computation in part 1) can be carried out by M'_H on $\log n$-tape and since for large j

$$|f(M_0 \# 0^j)| > |M_0 \# x|^{1/(k_0+1)}$$

we see that for

$$w_j = f(M_0 \# 0^j),$$

$$|w_j|^{k_0+1} > |M_0 \# 0^j|$$

and M'_H halts in step 1). Since the set $\{w_j | j \geqq 1\}$ is infinite, we see that there exists an infinite subset of H which is accepted on $\log n$-tape; as was to be shown. □

For related results about complete sets defined for *DCSL*'s under linear-time reductions see [3].

On the other hand, it is quite easy to construct infinite deterministic-context sensitive languages which have no infinite subsets which are easy to recognize. This shows that there exist everywhere hard to recognize sets in *DCSL* which, because of Theorem 4.4, are not L-complete.

THEOREM 4.5. *There exists an infinite language C in DCSL such that if $B \subseteqq C$, $|B| = \infty$ and $L(M_i) = C$, then*

$$\liminf_{n\to\infty} \frac{L_i(n)}{n} > 0.$$

Proof. The infinite language C is constructed by diagonalization in linear tape over all M_i such that

$$L_i(n) < n/|M_i| \quad \text{i.o.} \quad \square$$

As mentioned previously, one of the outstanding open problems in computational complexity is to decide whether

$$P = NP.$$

At the same time, if we assume that $P \neq NP$ then we can show that there exist sets in $NP - P$ which are not L-complete in NP [32].

THEOREM 4.6. *If $P \neq NP$ then there exist sets in $NP - P$ which are not L-complete.*

Proof. We will show that if a recursive set B is not in P then we can effectively construct a set A such that:

1. A is not in P,
2. $A \leqq_L B$,
3. $B \nleqq_L A$.

Thus if B is in $NP - P$ then A is a set in $NP - P$ which is not L-complete, since B in NP cannot be L-reduced to A.

The set A is defined in terms of B by an L-transducer, M_A, to be constructed below, as follows:

$$M_A(\Sigma^*) \subseteqq \{1\}^*,$$

$$M_A(w) = M_A(z) \quad \text{if } |w| = |z|,$$

$$A = \{w | w \in B \text{ and } |M_A(w)| \text{ is even}\}.$$

To see that $A \leqq_L B$ we observe that $B \neq \Sigma^*$ (else B is in P) and let $x_0 \in \Sigma^* - B$. Then A is reduced to B by an L-transducer M_B, such that

$$M_B(x) = \textbf{if } M_A(x) \text{ even } \textbf{then } x \textbf{ else } x_0.$$

Discussion of L-transducer M_A. Let $P_0, P_1, P_2, \ldots$ be an enumeration of the sets in P and let $M_i, M_2, M_3, \ldots$ be an enumeration of all L-transducers. Then we must have for all i:

$$A \neq P_i \quad \text{and} \quad [M_i(B) \not\subseteq A \text{ or } M_i(\bar{B}) \not\subseteq \bar{A}].$$

To achieve this M_A will be so constructed that it satisfies these conditions for all i. For example, to satisfy $A \neq P_i$, M_A will output for a while 1^{2i} (assuming it is processing elements of Σ^* in their natural order), making A look like B, until an x is found which shows that $P_i \neq B$ and therefore $P_i \neq A$; to satisfy the second condition M_A will output for a while 1^{2i+1}, making A look finite, until an x is found which shows that M_i does not L-reduce B to A (such x exists since otherwise $B \in P$). To implement this process on $\log n$-tape we will just delay certifying that the ith condition is met until M_A has enough tape to find the desired witnesses.

Construction of M_A. $M_A(\lambda) = \lambda$, where λ is the null string. For input w, $|w| = n \geqq 1$, M_A reconstructs on $\log n$-tape as much as possible of the sequence $M_A(\lambda), M_A(0), M_A(0^2), \ldots$; let $M_A(0^m)$ be the last member of this sequence reconstructed.

If $|M_A(0^m)|$ is even then let

$$i = |M_A(0^m)|/2$$

and on $\log n$-tape try to find a z such that $A(z) \neq P_i(z)$. If no such z is found print 1^{2i}, thus not certifying that $A \neq P_i$ has been verified, else print 1^{2i+1} verifying that $A \neq P_i$.

If $|M_A(0^m)|$ is odd then let

$$i = (|M_A(0^m)| - 1)/2$$

and on $\log n$-tape try to find a z which shows that M_i does not reduce B to A, i.e. $z \in B$ and $M_i(z) \notin A$ or vice versa. If no such z is found, print 1^{2i+1}, otherwise, print 1^{2i+2}.

Since in either case, the desired witnesses exist, they will be eventually found and M_A is seen to be an L-transducer satisfying the desired conditions. Thus

$$A \in NP - P$$

and A is not an L-complete set. □

It is still an open problem whether the assumption $P \neq NP$ implies that all L-complete sets in NP must have infinite L-recognizable subsets.

We recall that if M_{i_0} accepts the set

$$L_0 = \{M_i \# w \mid [(M_i \text{ rejects } w) \text{ or } (M_i \text{ uses more than } |M_i \# w|/|M_i| \text{ -tape})]\},$$

then the regular set

$$\{M_{i_0} \# w \mid w \in \Sigma^*\} \subseteq L_0$$

and M_{i_0} uses more than $|M_{i_0} \# w|/|M_{i_0}|$ tape on input $M_{i_0} \# w$. Thus the recognizer M_{i_0} can be effectively replaced by a recognizer $M_{\tau(i_0)}$ such that

$$L(M_{i_0}) = L(M_{\tau(i_0)}), \qquad L_{\tau(i_0)}(n) \leqq L_{i_0}(n)$$

and on the regular set $\{M_{i_0} \# w \mid w \in \Sigma^*\}$ on which M_{i_0} uses linear tape $M_{\tau(i_0)}$ uses no tape at all. Thus we see that any recognizer of the set L_0 can be effectively speeded-up on infinite subsets. Thus no optimal recognizers can exist for the set L_0.

In the following chapter we will show that such effective i.o. speed-up appears naturally in different applications.

CHAPTER 5

Long Proofs of Trivial Theorems

In this chapter we show that the use of proof methods similar to the ones exploited in the previous chapter yield a simple proof that in many interesting mathematical theories, for every formal (mechanical) proof method, there exists infinite sets of "trivially true" theorems which require as long proofs in the given formalism as the "hardest" theorems. Surprisingly, some of these infinite sets of trivially true theorems with long proofs can be found effectively for every given proof procedure and thus the proof procedure can be replaced by another one which shortens the proofs of infinitely many theorems without increasing the length of proofs for any others. For related work see [8], [19].

These results hold for many axiomatizable as well as decidable mathematical theories. They also show that there exist recursive functions and recursive sets for which every algorithm computing them can be effectively speeded-up infinitely often. Furthermore, these recursive functions appear naturally, and we observe that specific combinatorial problems fall in the class of problems for which every algorithm can be effectively speeded-up. Thus for many computations there do not exist optimal algorithms and every given one can be effectively speeded-up infinitely often.

These results show very clearly that we pay a price for formalizing mathematics. In every formalization, infinite sets of trivial theorems will require very long proofs. Thus we have a very dramatic and quantitative explanation why we should not and in practice do not freeze a formation when discussing or doing mathematics. They also give a warning that a necessarily long proof in a formal system does not certify that the result is nontrivial.

These observations are particularly interesting in view of the recent results about decision complexity of decidable mathematical theories, which show that many of these theories, though decidable, are not practically decidable. For example, it has been shown that for Pressburger arithmetic, the first order theory of natural numbers under addition, any proof procedure is such that the length of the proofs cannot be bounded by a double exponential in the length of the theorems [14]. Some even more dramatic complexity results are known about other decidable theories [41]. Our observation adds that not only are these theories very hard to decide, but that every decision procedure requires as much work (long proofs) as the hardest theorems in the theory on infinite sets of trivially true theorems and that from the description of the decision procedure, we can effectively obtain such infinite sets of trivially true theorems with long proofs. For related observations see also [41].

It is interesting to compare these results with the Blum speed-up theorem [7], [22]. We recall that Blum proved that for every recursive function g there exist recursive functions f for which any algorithm can be speeded up by the function g almost everywhere. Unfortunately, even if a function f has an almost everywhere speedup, the faster algorithm cannot be found effectively from a given algorithm, nor could one effectively compute from which point on the speed-up started. Finally, there is a widespread belief that functions with an almost everywhere speed-up are artificially constructed and that they do not appear naturally in mathematics or practical computing.

The situation with the functions, problems and mathematical theories which have speed-up infinitely often is quite different. This speed-up is effective and we can explicitly show subsets on which computations can be speeded-up. Furthermore, we do not have to construct artificial examples to show existence of such speed-up. The most important mathematical theories have, for every formalization, proof-shortening infinitely often, and many combinatorial problems which we are interested in solving are such that every algorithm can be speeded-up infinitely often. As a matter of fact, mathematical theories and sets which have speed-up infinitely often appear to be more natural than those which do not have such speed-up. See also [8], [41] and recall Theorem 4.4.

Finally, it is well known that the provable theorems of many important mathematical theories form creative sets [38]. One such mathematical theory is Peano arithmetic, which is based on Peano's axioms with those instances of the Peano induction axiom that can be expressed in elementary arithmetic. Several other well known examples can be easily found, and it is clear that the creative sets form a very important class of sets in mathematics [6], [38].

DEFINITION. An *axiomatizable theory* is a triple $F = (\Sigma, W, T)$ where

1. Σ is a finite nonempty alphabet,
2. W, $W \subseteq \Sigma^*$, is a recursive set, referred to as the set of *well-formed* formulas,
3. T, $T \subseteq W$, is a recursively enumerable set, referred to as set of *theorems provable* in F. If w is provable in F we will write

   $$\vdash_F w \quad \text{or} \quad \vdash w$$

   when F is fixed.

If the set T is recursive, the theory F is said to be *decidable.*

We can think of W as the syntactically correct formulas and T as the subset of these for which there exist proofs in the formal system F. (In practice we would prescribe a set of axioms and proof rules so that it can be recursively decided whether a given string following a well-formed formula is a proof of this formula).

We furthermore assume that the Turing machines form a model (or a submodel) for the theory F. Thus we assume that we can express and prove elementary facts about Turing machines in F and that only true statements about Turing machines can be proven in F; that is, F is sound.

We recall that a set A is creative iff A is an r.e. complete set; that is, A is an r.e. set to which any other r.e. set B can be reduced by a recursive mapping. Equivalently we can define creative sets in terms of productive sets [38].

DEFINITION. A set A is *creative* if A is r.e. and there exists a recursive function f such that

$$(\forall i)[L(M_i) \subseteq \bar{A} \text{ implies } f(i) \in \bar{A} - L(M_i)].$$

We also recall that all creative r.e. sets are recursively isomorphic.

Next we consider the difficulty of recognizing creative sets or equivalently the difficulty of proving theorems in mathematical theories, such as the Peano arithmetic. A natural measure of the difficulty of proving a theorem in a formal mathematical theory is the length of the shortest proof. Unfortunately, to do this, we have to know explicitly how the theory is axiomatized and what proof procedures are used. To avoid such unnecessary difficulties we will measure the difficulty of recognizing sets (of provable theorems) by the amount of tape used by Turing machines recognizing these sets. Intuitively, this measure can be justified by observing that for any (reasonable) proof procedure, we can design a Turing machine which for any given theorem successively checks all possible proofs of increasing length until it finds a proof of the given theorem (or never halts if the input is not a provable theorem). Clearly, the amount of tape used by this Turing machine is a lower bound for the length of the proof and corresponds, intuitively, directly to the amount of erasable blackboard space needed to verify the proof or present it. Consider the set

$$\begin{aligned} L_0 = \{(i, j, w) \mid\; & i, j \in N,\ w \in \Sigma^*, \\ & M_j \text{ or } M_i \text{ on input } (i, j, w) \text{ uses a finite amount of tape,} \\ & \text{and either } M_i \text{ does not accept } (i, j, w) \\ & \quad \text{or } M_i \text{ uses more tape than } M_j \text{ on } (i, j, w)\}, \end{aligned}$$

where i and j are binary representations of the corresponding integers and (i, j, w) is the sequence i, j, w enclosed in parentheses. We say that M_j uses more tape than M_i on input x if M_i uses a finite amount of tape and M_j uses at least one more tape square than M_i on input x.

We now show that the set L_0 is recursively enumerable. We observe that for any Turing machine M_i, input x and integer k, we can recursively decide whether M_i for input x uses more than k tape squares. If M_i uses less than k tape squares for input x we can decide whether x is accepted by M_i or not. Thus to enumerate L_0 we just reject all inputs which are not of the form (i, j, w). For input (i, j, w) we check successively for $k = 0, 1, 2, \ldots$ whether M_i or M_j uses exactly k tape squares for input (i, j, w). If it is found that one of the Turing machines uses a finite amount of tape then we can decide whether M_i uses more tape than M_j; if so, (i, j, w) is accepted. If M_i uses less tape than M_j then we can decide whether M_i accepts (i, j, w) and it is accepted iff M_i does not accept it.

LEMMA 5.1. *The set L_0 is a creative set.*

Proof. We known that L_0 is an r.e. set. To show that it is a creative set, let $M_{k'}$ be a Tm which simulates M_k and tests whether M_k uses a finite amount of tape; if M_k is found to use a finite amount of tape, then $M_{k'}$ accepts the input if M_k does not and vice versa. The function $f(k) = (k', k', w_0)$, for any fixed w_0 in Σ^*, is a productive function for the set L_0, since $L(M_k) \subseteq \bar{L}_0$ implies that (k', k', w_0) is in $\bar{L}_0 - L(M_k)$. Thus L_0 is a creative set, as was to be shown. □

THEOREM 5.2. *Let M_{i_0} recognize the set L_0, $L(M_{i_0}) = L_0$, and let M_{j_0} be a Turing machine which halts for all inputs. Then the regular set*

$$\{(i_0, j_0, w) | w \in \Sigma^*\}$$

is a subset of L_0 and, on every input (i_0, j_0, w), M_{i_0} uses no less tape than M_{j_0} on the same input.

Proof. Let (i_0, j_0, w) denote the sequence i_0, j_0, w enclosed in parentheses. Then, for fixed i_0 and j_0,

$$\{(i_0, j_0, w) | w \in \Sigma^*\}$$

is a regular set. Since M_{j_0} halts for all inputs we see that on every input (i_0, j_0, w) the Turing machine M_{i_0} uses no less tape than M_{j_0} on this input, because otherwise, if M_{i_0} accepts (i_0, j_0, w) using less tape than M_{j_0}, (i_0, j_0, w) would be in $L(M_{i_0})$ but not in L_0, which contradicts the assumption that $L(M_{i_0}) = L_0$. Similarly if M_{i_0} rejects (i_0, j_0, w), using less tape than M_{j_0} on this input, (i_0, j_0, w) would be in L_0 but not in $L(M_{i_0})$, which again is a contradiction. If M_{i_0} uses no less tape than M_{j_0} on (i_0, j_0, w) then M_{i_0} must accept the input, since otherwise we have the contradiction that (i_0, j_0, w) is in L_0 but not in $L(M_{i_0})$. Thus $\{(i_0, j_0, w) | w \in \Sigma^*\}$ is a subset of L_0 and on every element of this subset M_{i_0} uses no less tape than M_{j_0}. This completes the proof. □

From this result we immediately get the following.

COROLLARY 5.3. *For every Turing machine which recognizes L_0 and every recursive function f we can effectively find an infinite regular subset of L_0 on which for each input of length n, M_{i_0} uses at least $f(n)$ tape squares for its recognition.*

If the members of L_0 are considered as provable theorems of a mathematical theory, the result asserts that every formalization of this mathematical theory will have infinite sets of "trivially" true theorems but which in the formalism require horrendously long proofs.

To illustrate this, assume that we have a first order mathematical theory with the standard logical connectives and in which we can express such concepts as

"M_i uses less tape than M_j on input x"

and

"M_i does not accept the input x."

Assume that the theory is strong enough to prove all true statements of the form

"M_j or M_i uses a finite amount of tape on input (i, j, w) and, either M_i does not accept (i, j, w) or M_i uses more tape than M_j on (i, j, w)."

For example, the Peano arithmetic is such a mathematical theory.

From our previous result we see that any proof procedure for this mathematical theory will have easily recognizable infinite sets of true theorems such that the length of their shortest proofs in the given formalism will grow faster than any given recursive function (of the length of the theorems to be proved).

We observe that these results hold for all creative sets.

COROLLARY 5.4. *Let B be a creative set, let M_i be a Turing machine which recognizes B and let f be a recursive function. Then we can effectively find an infinite recursive subset of B which can be recognized by a Turing machine using $L(n)$-tape but on which the Turing machine M_i uses at least $f \circ L(n)$-tape.*

Proof. This follows from the fact that all creative sets are recursively isomorphic and that the recursive isomorphic function can be computed on a recursively bounded amount of tape. □

The family of recursively enumerable sets which have effective speed-up of the type we proved for creative sets has been completely characterized in [8], and Corollary 5.4 follows from this general characterization, though these proofs are quite complicated.

We now derive related results for decidable theories. Let $L_i(n)$ be the maximal number of tape squares used by the Tm M_i on inputs of length n. We say that a total function $L(n)$ is *tape constructible* iff there exists a Tm M_i such that $L(n)=L_i(n)$.

THEOREM 5.5. *For every tape comstructible $L(n)\geqq n$ there exists a recursive set A_L (a recursive function $f_L: \Sigma^* \to \{0, 1\}$) such that*

1. *A_L can be recognized on $L(n)$-tape but not on $L_1(n)$-tape if*

$$\lim_{n\to\infty} \frac{L_1(n)}{L(n)} = 0,$$

2. *for every M_{i_0} such that $L(M_{i_0}) = A_L$ we can effectively find an infinite regular subset R_{i_0} of A_L such that M_{i_0} uses at least $L(n)/|M_{i_0}|$-tape on every member of R_{i_0}.*

Proof. Let $M_1, M_2, \ldots$ be a standard enumeration of all one-tape Tm's such that the set $\{M_i\}$ is recognizable in polynomial time on linear tape. Let $L(n)\geqq n$ be tape constructible and let

$$A_L = \{(M_i, w) | M_i \text{ does not accept } (M_i, w) \text{ on } L(|(M_i, w)|)/|M_i|\text{-tape}\}.$$

Note that (M_i, w) is in A_L if either M_i uses more than $L(|M_i, w)|)/|M_i|$-tape or it does not accept the input on this amount of tape. We claim that A_L is $L(n)$-tape acceptable by the following method: for input x, check if x is of the form (M_i, w); if not, reject. For input (M_i, w), lay off $L(|M_i, w)|)$-tape and on a separate track of the tape simulate M_i on input (M_i, w); accept it if the simulation tries to use more than $L(|M_i, w)|)/|M_i|$-tape. If the simulation halts on the available tape, reject it if accepted and vice versa. Clearly, this simulation can be carried out on $L(|(M_i, w)|)$-tape and we see that A_L is $L(n)$-tape acceptable.

Let M_{i_0} be a recognizer of A_L and consider the regular set

$$R_{i_0} = \{(M_{i_0}, w) | w \in \Sigma^*\}.$$

The Tm M_{i_0} on input (M_{i_0}, w) either uses more than $L(|(M_{i_0}, w)|)/|M_{i_0}|$-tape or it does not. If it does then (M_{i_0}, w) is in $L(M_{i_0})$. If it does not then either (M_{i_0}, w) is accepted or not. In either case, we get a contradiction: if (M_{io}, w) is accepted then (M_{io}, w) is in $L(M_{io})$ but not in A_L contradicting $L(M_{io}) = A_L$; if (M_{io}, w) is not accepted then (M_{io}, w) is in A_L but not in $L(M_{io})$, again contradicting the assumption $L(M_{io}) = A_L$. Thus we must conclude that $R_{io} \subseteq A_L$ and that on all inputs (M_{io}, w) the machine M_{io} uses more than $L(|(M_{io}, w)|)/|M_{io}|$-tape. From this it also follows that A_L is recognizable on $L_1(n)$-tape, provided

$$\lim_{n \to \infty} \frac{L_1(n)}{L(n)} = 0.$$

This completes the proof. □

Next we show that many decidable mathematical theories must have trivial theorems requiring long proofs and that we can effectively find infinite sets of such trivial theorems with long proofs.

Let F be a consistent, decidable mathematical theory, let L and T be tape constructible functions such that for all n, $T(n+1) > T(n) \geqq n$ and $L(n) \geqq n$. Let there exist a Tm M which for input (M_i, w) writes a formula $\gamma_{i,w}$ in F such that:

1. $\gamma_{i,w}$ is provable in F iff $(M_i, w) \in A_L$, that is, iff the Turing machine M_i does not accept input (M_i, w) on $L(|M_i, w)|)/|M_i|$-tape.
2. $|\gamma_{i,w}| \leqq T(|(M_i, w)|)$ and M use no more than $|\gamma_{i,w}|$-tape to write $\gamma_{i,w}$ for input (M_i, w).

COROLLARY 5.6. *Any decision procedure for the theory F requires at least $L \circ T^{-1}(n)$-tape and for every Turing machine M_{io} which recognizes the theorems of F we can effectively find an infinite subset F' of theorems of F such that F' is recognizable on linear tape but M_{io} uses at least $c \cdot L \circ T^{-1}(n)$-tape on every element of F', for a constant $c > 0$.*

Proof. Let M_{io} recognize the theorems of F. We now convert M_{io} to a recognizer of A_L, M_{ioo}. For input x, M_{ioo} checks if $x = (M_i, w)$; if not, it is rejected. For input (M_i, w), the machine M_{ioo} computes $\gamma_{i,w}$ and applies M_{io} to $\gamma_{i,w}$. Clearly, M_{ioo} accepts A_L. Assume now that M_{io} operates on L_{io}-tape such that

$$\lim_{n \to \infty} \frac{L_{io}(n)}{L \circ T^{-1}(n)} = 0.$$

Then M_{ioo} would operate on $L_{io}[T(n)]$-tape; but then

$$\lim_{n \to \infty} \frac{L_{io}[T(n)]}{L \circ T^{-1} \circ T(n)} = \lim_{n \to \infty} \frac{L_{io}[T(n)]}{L(n)} = 0,$$

which contradicts the fact that no such recognizer exists for A_L.

We now show how to obtain the set F' using M_{ioo}. We know that the regular set

$$R = \{(M_{ioo}, w) | w \in \Sigma^*\}$$

is a subset of A_L and that M_{ioo} uses at least $L(n)/|M_{ioo}|$-tape on inputs from R. We let

$$F' = \{\gamma_{ioo,w} | w \in \Sigma^*\};$$

clearly, F' is an infinite set of true theorems of F. To recognize the set F' we proceed as follows: for input γ (on track below γ) check for (M_{io_0}, w), $|(M_{io_0}, w)| \leqq |\gamma|$, whether $\gamma = \gamma_{io_0,w}$.

If no such (M_{io_0}, w) is found, reject the input; otherwise accept it. Clearly, F' is recognizable on linear tape, since $|\gamma_{i,w}| \geqq |(M_i, w)|$, and the computation of $\gamma_{i,w}$ from (M_i, w) requires no more than $|\gamma_{i,w}|$-tape. On the other hand, since M_{io_0} uses $L(n)/|M_{io_0}|$-tape on R, M_{io} must use at least $L \circ T^{-1}(n)/|M_{io_0}|$-tape, since $|\gamma_{io_0,w}| \leqq T(|(M_{io_0}, w)|)$. This completes the proof. □

Recent work on the complexity of decision procedures for decidable mathematical theories has shown how statements about Turing machine computations can be efficiently encoded in formulas in these theories so that the statement about the Tm computation is true iff the formula is provable in the theory [1], [25], [41], [42]. These results can be used not only to establish the complexity of the decision procedures, but also the existence of i.o. speed-up for most of these decision procedures [19], [41].

For example, it has been shown [41] that the set

$$\mathcal{R} = \{R \mid R \text{ is a regular expression over } \Sigma, \cdot, \cup, \neg, {}^*,), (, \text{ and } L(R) = \varnothing\}$$

cannot be recognized on tape bounded by an elementary function. By the same techniques it follows that every Tm recognizing this set can be effectively speeded-up by any desired "stack of exponentials" on infinite subsets of $\mathcal{R}$.

We conclude with a look at time complexity of decision procedures and speed-up of proofs for Pressburger arithmetic [14].

Let $T_i(n)$ be the maximal number of steps taken by the Tm M_i on inputs of length n. We say that $T(n)$ is *time constructible* iff $T(n)$ is computable in $T(n)$ steps.

COROLLARY 5.7. *Let $T(n) \geqq n^2$ be time constructible. Then there exists a set A_T,*

$$A_T = \left\{(M_i, w) \,\middle|\, M_i \text{ does not accept } (M_i, w) \text{ in time } \frac{T(n)}{|M_i| \log T(n)}\right\},$$

such that A_T is recognizable in time $T(n)$ and if $L(M_{io}) = A_T$ then the regular set

$$R = \{(M_{io}, w) \mid w \in \Sigma^*\},$$

is a subset of A_T and M_{io} uses at least

$$\frac{T(n)}{|M_{io}| \log T(n)}$$

steps for every member of R.

Proof. Similar to the proof of Theorem 5.5. The one difference is in the factor $\log T(n)$ which appears because we have to use a less efficient simulation algorithm than in the tape complexity case [18]. With the use of [36] the $\log T(n)$ factor can be replaced by $\log^* T(n)$. □

We recall that the Pressburger arithmetic (PA) is the first order theory of addition of natural numbers. This theory is decidable and it "is one of the simplest, most basic, imaginable mathematical theories" [14]. Furthermore, it has been shown that any nondeterministic Tm recognizing the true theorems of PA must use at least time

$$T(n) = 2^{2^{cn}} \quad \text{for some } c > 0.$$

From this, one concludes that any "reasonable" proof procedure for PA will have theorems of length n whose shortest proof must be longer than $2^{2^{cn}}$ [14].

We add to this result the following observation.

THEOREM 5.8. *Let M_{io} be a Turing machine which recognizes the theorems of PA. Then we can effectively find an infinite set T of theorems of PA such that T is recognizable in polynomial time but M_{io} uses at least time*

$$T(n) \geqq 2^{2^{qn}}, \quad \text{for some } q > 0,$$

for every element of T.

Proof. By a close inspection of the proof techniques used in [14] and using reasoning similar to that in the proof of Corollaries 5.6 and 5.7, we can construct the set T' of sentences $\gamma_{io,w}$ in PA asserting that M_{io} does not accept the input $(M_{io,w})$ in time

$$\frac{2^{2^{dn}}}{|M_{io}| \log (2^{2^{dn}})} = \frac{2^{2^{dn}}}{2^{dn}|M_{io}|}, \quad \text{for some } d > 0.$$

From this we then conclude that for some $q > 0$ and sufficiently large n:

$$\frac{2^{2^{dn}}}{2^{dn}|M_{io}|} \geqq 2^{2^{qn}}.$$

Thus, the recognition of the set T' by M_{io} requires at least $2^{2^{qn}}$ steps for almost all elements of T'. By removing the short elements of T' we get the desired set T. On the other hand, it can be seen from [14] that the set T is recognizable in polynomial time. This completes the proof. □

Thus again we see that for this very basic and simple theory we can effectively find, for every proof procedure, infinite sets of theorems which are recognizable as true in polynomial time, but for which the shortest proofs in the formalism are horrendously long. Again the limitations of formal methods and mechanical proof procedures, even for this very simple mathematical theory, have been pointed out.

CHAPTER 6

What Can and Cannot Be Proven About Computational Complexity

In this section we consider the problem of what can and cannot be formally proven about complexity of computations and complexity classes.

This work is motivated by the current interest in computer science in proving properties of programs and by the general desire to understand better what can and cannot be proven formally about the complexity of computations. *As we will see in this chapter, the results about complexity of computations change quite radically if we consider only properties of computations which can be proven formally.* As a matter of fact, these results suggest that we must adjust our intuitive ideas about computational complexity in view of these results and, we believe, that this problem area deserves a thorough investigation [17], [20], [44].

We first look at the problem of proving sharp time bounds for the running times of one-tape (k-tape) Turing machines and relate this problem to a fundamental problem about what can and cannot be formally proven about computational complexity classes [20].

An important problem in computational complexity theory is to determine, for a given computer model and computer resource, how much a given resource bound $T(n)$ (satisfying some honesty conditions) has to be increased to be able to compute something new which cannot be computed in the old resource bound $T(n)$.

The standard way to obtain separation results for complexity classes is by efficiently diagonalizing over all the computations which can be performed in the given resource bound. The efficiency of the diagonal process over the resource bounded computations, or the additional amount of resources required to carry out the diagonalization over all the computations computable within the given resource bound, determines the sharpness of the results. The usual way to carry out such diagonal processes is to bound the given resource as a function of the length of the input and by simulation determine on successive inputs what different Turing machines do and do the opposite, provided their simulation did not try to exceed the given resource bound [18], [20], [27]. Such diagonal processes, in essence, require that we perform two separate computations: a simulation process and a process which shuts the computation off if it tries to use too much of the bounded resource.

This method works very well for reusable resource measures where we can first compute the resource bound and then perform the simulation within the bounded resources. For example, for the tape bounded Turing machine computations the following result holds [22], [27].

THEOREM 6.1. *Let $t(n)$, $t(n) \geqq \log n$, be computable on $t(n)$-tape. Then*

$$\lim_{n\to\infty} \frac{t_1(n)}{t(n)} = 0.$$

implies that $TAPE[L_1(n)] \subsetneqq TAPE[L(n)]$.

For time bounded Turing machine computations the problems become more difficult and the results depend on whether we consider the class of all many-tape Turing machines or the class of one-tape Turing machines [18], [22], [27], [36].

For one-tape Turing machines (or Turing machines with a fixed number of tapes), the simulation of one-tape machines on a fixed one-tape machine can be carried out without a substantial time loss, but the running of the shut-off "clock" must be performed (in parallel) with the simulations operations on the same tape (or the fixed number of tapes). The combining of two independent computations on one tape leads to a time loss, and the best result about one-tape Turing machines known up to the present is stated below [18].

THEOREM 6.2. *Let $T(n) \geqq n \log n$ be computable on* $\log T(n)$*-tape in $T(n)$ time by a one-tape Turing machine. Then*

$$\lim_{n\to\infty} \frac{T_1(n)}{T(n)} = 0.$$

implies that $TIME[T_1(n)] \subsetneqq TIME[T(n) \cdot \log T(n)]$.

It is seen from the last result that the need to carry along a "clock" does not permit us (so far) to prove for time bounded computations of one-tape Turing machines as sharp results as we have for the tape-bounded computations and which we conjecture also hold for time bounded computations.

In this chapter we study a new class of diagonalization processes over resource bounded classes in which we do not use (explicitly) a "clock". In particular, we study the class of diagonal processes over time-bounded computations of one-tape (or k-tape) Turing machines in which we diagonalize over the computations of a Turing machine M_i only if there is a formal proof that M_i runs in the given time bound. Thus in these diagonal processes we replace the "clock" which shuts off the simulation before it takes too much time by a formal proof that the simulation will not take too much time. As we will show, this approach will establish close links between properties of proof systems and the existence of sharp time bounds for one-tape Turing machine computations. Thus these results raise some interesting questions about what can and cannot be proven formally about running times of computations and emphasize the importance of these problems to computational complexity theory.

In this discussion let $M_1, M_2, M_3, \ldots$ be a standard enumeration of one-tape Tm's.

DEFINITION. The *complexity classes* and *provable complexity classes* are defined for partial recursive functions $T(n)$ as follows:

$$TIME[T(n)] = \{L(M_i) \mid T_i(n) \leqq T(n)\}$$

and

$$F\text{-}TIME[T(n)] = \{L(M_i) | \text{“}T_i(n) \leqq T(n)\text{” is provable in } F\}$$
$$= \{L(M_i) | \vdash_F T_i(n) \leqq T(n)\}.$$

Thus the class $TIME[T(n)]$ is the class of all sets acceptable by one-tape Tm's whose running time is bounded by $T(n)$, without specifying how to determine that this is so. On the other hand, for a fixed formal system F the class $F\text{-}TIME[T(n)]$ is the complexity class consisting of the languages accepted by Tm's for which there is a proof in F that they run in the time bound $T(n)$.

For related work on provable properties of computational complexity problems see [17], [44] and for early work on provable recursive functions see [15].

THEOREM 6.3. *Let $T(n)$, $T(n) \geqq n \cdot \log n$, be a recursive function for which*

$$F\text{-}TIME[T(n)] = TIME[T(n)].$$

Then for any nondecreasing, unbounded recursive function $g(n)$, $g(n) \geqq 1$, we have that

$$TIME[T(n)] \neq TIME[T(n) \cdot g(n)].$$

Proof. Since $g(n) \geqq 1$ we know that

$$TIME[T(n)] \subseteq TIME[T(n) \cdot g(n)].$$

To show that

$$TIME[T(n)] \neq TIME[T(n) \cdot g(n)]$$

we construct a Tm M_D such that

$$L(M_D) \in TIME[T(n) \cdot g(n)] - TIME[T(n)].$$

The machine M_D operates as follows:

1. For input x, M_D lays off $\log \log |x|$-tape in $|x| \cdot \log |x|$ steps and checks if x has the format

$$x = x_1 \# x_2 \# x_3$$

with x_1, x_2, x_3 in $(\Sigma - \#)^*$ and such that

$$|x_1 \# x_2 \#| \leqq \log \log |x|.$$

If not the input is rejected; otherwise:

2. M_D checks whether x_1 is a description of a Tm, say M_i, and x_2 is a proof in F that $T_i(n) \leqq T(n)$ for all n (for a fixed Tm, M_{i_0}, computing $T(n)$). If not, the input is rejected; otherwise:
3. On the marked-off tape M_D searches for m such that

$$1 \leqq m \leqq n \quad \text{and} \quad |x_1|^2 \leqq g(m).$$

If no such m is found, the input is rejected; otherwise:

4. M_D simulates $x_1 = M_i$ on input

$$x = x_1 \# x_2 \# x_3$$

and accepts x iff M_i rejects it.

Note that the steps 1, 2 and 3 can all be carried out in time $n \cdot \log n$ for $n = |x|$, since $\log \log n$-tape can be layed-off in $n \cdot \log n$ steps; and since all the other processes halt and are carried out on $\log \log n$-tape, the total time is bounded by $n \cdot \log n$ for these steps. Since we can only prove true properties about Turing machines in F, we know that successful completion of step 2 guarantees that M_i runs in time $T_i(n) \leqq T(n)$. Furthermore, since we can simulate a step of M_i computation in $|x_1|^2$ steps on M_D, the condition $|x_1|^2 \leqq g(m)$ for some $m \leqq n$ implies that $|x_1|^2 \leqq g(n)$ and therefore M_D operates in time

$$T_D(n) \leqq T_i(n) \cdot g(n) \leqq T(n) \cdot g(n).$$

Thus

$$L(M_D) \text{ is in } \mathit{TIME}[T(n) \cdot g(n)].$$

On the other hand, $L(M_D)$ cannot be in $F\text{-}\mathit{TIME}[T(n)]$ since this would imply that there exists a Tm M_i such that $L(M_i) = L(M_D)$ and there is a proof in the formal system F that $T_i(n) \leqq T(n)$ and therefore we must have that $L(M_i) \neq L(M_D)$. Thus $L(M_i)$ is not in $F\text{-}\mathit{TIME}[T(n)]$, and because of our hypotheses we know that

$$L(M_D) \in \mathit{TIME}[T(n) \cdot g(n)] - \mathit{TIME}[T(n)],$$

as was to be shown. □

From the proof of Theorem 6.3 it immediately follows that for any recursive time bound, a "slight" increase in the bound permits a new computation which is not provably computable in the old complexity bound.

COROLLARY 6.4. *Let $T(n)$, $T(n) \geqq n \cdot \log n$, be a recursive function and let $g(n) \geqq 1$ be a nondecreasing, unbounded recursive function. Then*

$$F\text{-}\mathit{TIME}[T(n)] \subsetneqq \mathit{TIME}[T(n) \cdot g(n)].$$

Proof. The corollary follows immediately from Theorem 6.4. □

The above theorem shows that the condition

$$F\text{-}\mathit{TIME}[T(n)] = \mathit{TIME}[T(n)]$$

yields very sharp hierarchy results for time-bounded one-tape Tm computations. This leaves a very interesting open problem about the validity of the assumption

$$F\text{-}\mathit{TIME}[T(n)] = \mathit{TIME}[T(n)].$$

We conjecture that this condition holds for time bounds with certain "honesty" conditions. For example, the previous diagonalization results [18] required that the time bound $T(n)$ be computable in time $T(n)$ and on $\log T(n)$-

tape. Thus we would expect that

$$F\text{-}TIME[T(n)] = TIME[T(n)]$$

for such functions as

$$T(n) = n \log n, \quad T(n) = n^2, \quad T(n) = 2^n, \quad \text{etc.}$$

Later in this chapter we will show that the corresponding conjecture holds for tape-bounded computations for which we can, in essence, show that a complexity class is equal to the corresponding provable complexity class iff the complexity class can be defined by a tape constructible bound.

On the other hand, our next result shows there exist recursive time bounds for which the classic complexity classes differ from the corresponding provable complexity classes. That is, we will show that there exist recursive, monotonically increasing functions $T(n)$ such that for some set A acceptable in time $T(n)$ there is no Tm M_i which accepts A and for which it can be proven in F that $T_i(n) \leqq T(n)$.

Though this theorem is only stated for one-tape Tm's, it is easily seen that it holds for all computational complexity measures [7].

THEOREM 6.5. *There exist recursive, monotonically increasing time bounds $T(n)$ such that*

$$F\text{-}TIME[T(n)] \neq TIME[T(n)].$$

Proof. By the gap theorem [9], [22] we can effectively construct a recursive, monotonically increasing function $T_0(n) \geqq n \cdot \log n$ such that

$$TIME[T_0(n)] = TIME[T_0(n)^2].$$

But by Theorem 6.3 we know that, choosing $g(n) = T_0(n)$, we get

$$F\text{-}TIME[T_0(n)] \neq TIME[T_0(n)^2].$$

Thus

$$F\text{-}TIME[T_0(n)] \neq TIME[T_0(n)],$$

as was to be shown. □

By similar reasoning we can get the next independence result about nonexistence of formal proofs of resource bounds.

COROLLARY 6.6. *Let $G(n)$ be a nondecreasing, unbounded recursive function. Then there exist arbitrarily large, nondecreasing recursive functions $T(n)$ such that for any formal system F (satisfying our assumptions)*

$$F\text{-}TIME[G(T(n))] \subsetneqq TIME[T(n)].$$

It should be observed that for every formal mathematical system F we can effectively construct a recursive bound $T(n)$ such that for each provably total M_i the running time $T_i(n) \leqq T(n)$ for sufficiently large n.

Note, though, that the proofs of Theorem 6.5 and Corollary 6.6 are not based on such a size argument. The time bound $T_0(n)$ of Theorem 6.5 is such that for any formal mathematical system F (satisfying our previous assumptions) we must have

$$F\text{-}TIME[T_0(n)] \neq TIME[T_0(n)].$$

Thus we see that for the time bound $T_0(n)$, yielded by the gap theorem, for every formal system F there will be a set A and there will be Tm's accepting A in time $T_0(n)$, but for none of these machines can it be proven in F that they run in time $T_0(n)$. This effect is strengthened by Corollary 6.6.

From the above we see that though the time bound $T_0(n)$ is effectively constructed the complexity class defined by $T_0(n)$ is such that we cannot effectively list names of Tm's which accept these sets and run in time $T_0(n)$. *Thus we see that the originally surprising gap theorem describes a fact about nonconstructive complexity classes. Or, stated differently, it is a result about a class of languages whose defining properties cannot be verified formally.*

Our next result shows that a gap result can hold for provable complexity classes for a formal system F only if they differ from the corresponding nonconstructively defined complexity classes and, furthermore, that we can constructively exhibit a set on which they differ. As a matter of fact, a gap in the provable complexity classes implies that there is no proof in F that, the simply constructed Tm M_D of Theorem 6.3 runs in time $T(n) \cdot g(n)$, nor is there a proof in F, for any other M_i for which $L(M_i) = L(M_D)$, that

$$T_i(n) \leqq T(n) \cdot g(n).$$

COROLLARY 6.7. *For a recursive function $T(n)$, $T(n) \geqq n \cdot \log n$, and a nondecreasing, unbounded recursive function $g(n)$, $g(n) \geqq 1$, we can have a gap in the hierarchy of the provable complexity classes,*

$$F\text{-}TIME[T(n)] = F\text{-}TIME[T(n) \cdot g(n)],$$

only if

$$F\text{-}TIME[T(n) \cdot g(n)] \subsetneqq TIME[T(n) \cdot g(n)]$$

and we can effectively construct a set A such that

$$A \in TIME[T(n) \cdot g(n)] = F\text{-}TIME[T(n) \cdot g(n)].$$

Proof. From our assumption about F we know that

$$F\text{-}TIME[T(n) \cdot g(n)] \subseteq TIME[T(n) \cdot g(n)],$$

from Theorem 6.3 we know that

$$F\text{-}TIME[T(n)] \neq TIME[T(n) \cdot g(n)],$$

and therefore

$$F\text{-}TIME[T(n)] \subsetneqq TIME[T(n) \cdot g(n)].$$

Furthermore we know that for the effectively constructed Tm M_D of Theorem 6.3 we have

$$L(M_D) \in TIME[T(n) \cdot g(n)],$$

and from the hypotheses of this theorem it follows that

$$L(M_D) \in TIME[T(n) \cdot g(n)] - F\text{-}TIME[T(n) \cdot g(n)],$$

as was to be shown. □

If it can be proven in F for M_D of Theorem 6.3 that

$$T_D(n) \leqq T(n) \cdot g(n),$$

then, as the next result shows, there are no gaps between provable complexity classes.

COROLLARY 6.8. *If it can be shown in F that the Turing machine M_D constructed in the proof of Theorem* 6.3 *runs in time*

$$T_D(n) \leqq T(n) \cdot g(n)$$

(which we know is true), *then*

$$F\text{-}TIME[T(n)] \neq F\text{-}TIME[T(n) \cdot g(n)].$$

Proof. The proof is obvious. □

To gain some further insight into when complexity classes are equal to the corresponding provable complexity classes and into what can and cannot be proven about complexity of computations, we consider tape-bounded computations. As in many other cases, it turns out that we can prove sharper results for tape-bounded computations than for time-bounded computations.

Recall that $L_i(n)$ denotes the maximum amount of tape used by a Tm M_i on inputs of length n. Let us fix a Tm, M_{i_0}, which computes the recursive function $T(n)$, then

$$TAPE[T(n)] = \{L(M_i) | L_i(n) \leqq T(n)\}$$

and

$$F\text{-}TAPE[T(n)] = \{L(M_i) | \vdash_F L_i(n) \leqq T(n)\}.$$

We recall that a function $T(n)$ is *tape constructible* iff there exists a Tm M which for input of length n lays off exactly $T(n)$ tape squares without using more than $T(n)$-tape.

In the next result we will consider all one tape Tm's with a fixed tape alphabet $\Sigma = \Sigma_0$ and denote the corresponding complexity classes by

$$TAPE_{\Sigma_0}[T(n)] \text{ and } F\text{-}TAPE_{\Sigma_0}[T(n)].$$

Our next result shows that in essence a tape-bounded complexity class coincides with the corresponding provable complexity class if and only if the class can be defined by a tape constructible bound.

Note that the following result asserts for tape bounded computations that if a set is accepted by some Tm M_i which runs on $L_i(n)$-tape then this fact can be proven formally in F. Surprisingly, the corresponding result for time-bounded one-tape Turing machines is not known to be true.

THEOREM 6.9. 1. *If $t(n) \geqq n$ is tape constructible then*

$$TAPE[t(n)] = F\text{-}TAPE[t(n)].$$

2. *If $TAPE_{\Sigma_0}[T(n)] = F\text{-}TAPE_{\Sigma_0}[T(n)]$ $(T(n) \geqq n)$ then there exists a tape constructible $t(n)$ such that*

$$TAPE_{\Sigma_0}[T(n)] = TAPE_{\Sigma_0}[t(n)].$$

Proof. Since $t(n)$ is tape constructible and we can prove elementary facts about Turing machines in the formal system F, there exists a Tm M_{i_t} with the following properties:

1) For any input of length n, the Tm M_{i_t} lays off exactly $t(n)$ tape squares without using more than $t(n)$-tape.
2) M_{i_t} halts for all inputs w such that $t(|w|)$ is finite.
3) It is provable in F that M_{i_t} computes a (partial recursive) tape constructible function.

Properties 1) and 2) follow from the definition of a tape constructible function and elementary facts about detecting cycling for tape bounded computations. Property 3) follows from the fact that M_{i_t} can be so chosen that from inspection of its description it is clear that it can only halt after printing a "1" on each tape square it has visited except the leftmost and rightmost squares which are marked with "#". Thus it is provable in F that M_{i_t} computes a tape constructible function. It is not necessarily provable in F that $t(n)$ is a total function, but that is not needed for our proof.

Using the machine M_{i_t} (as a subroutine to lay off the desired amount of tape) we can effectively construct for any i a Tm $M_{\tau(i)}$ with the following properties:

1. $M_{\tau(i)}$ rejects input w if M_i on w uses more than $t(|w|)$-tape; otherwise, $M_{\tau(i)}$ accepts w iff M_i accepts.
2. It is provable in F that $M_{\tau(i)}$ uses no more tape than M_{i_t}.

Thus we conclude that for a tape constructible $t(n)$ for every M_i which runs on tape $t(n)$ there exists an equivalent Tm $M_{\tau(i)}$ which provably in F uses no more than $t(n)$-tape. Thus

$$TAPE[t(n)] = F\text{-}TAPE[t(n)].$$

Conversely, if

$$TAPE_{\Sigma_0}[T(n)] = F\text{-}TAPE_{\Sigma_0}[T(n)]$$

then we can effectively enumerate the set of Tm's (with tape alphabet Σ_0)

$$\{M_{i_j} \mid \vdash_F L_{i_j}(n) \leqq T(n)\} = \{M_{i_j} \mid j \in I\}.$$

But then it follows that the function

$$t(n) = \max \{\{n\} \cup \{L_{i_j}(n) | M_{i_j} \text{ is enumerated on } n \text{ tape}\}$$

is tape constructible since we can simulate all enumerated M_{i_j} on $L_{i_j}(n)$ tape and find the maximum. Note that the machine computing $t(n)$ may have a larger tape alphabet than Σ_0. Further, we can see that

$$t(n) \leqq T(n)$$

and if

$$L(M_i) \in TAPE_{\Sigma_0}[T(n)]$$

then there exists an equivalent M_{i_j} with

$$\vdash_F L_{i_j}(n) \leqq T(n)$$

and therefore

$$L_{i_j}(n) \leqq t(n) \quad \text{a.e.}$$

But then there exists an equivalent Tm M_s such that $L_s(n) \leqq t(n)$ for all n. Thus

$$TAPE_{\Sigma_0}[t(n)] = TAPE_{\Sigma_0}[T(n)]$$

as was to be shown. □

From the previous result it follows immediately that if some set A is accepted on a tape bound achieved by a Tm then this fact can be proven in F.

COROLLARY 6.10. *For every (total) M_i with $L_i(n) \geqq n$*

$$TAPE[L_i(n)] = F\text{-}TAPE[L_i(n)].$$

Proof. The proof is obvious. □

It should be pointed out that it is not known whether the corresponding result holds for time bounded Turing machines. The best known result for one-tape Tm's follows from [18].

COROLLARY 6.11. *For every (total) one-tape Turing machine M_i*

$$TIME[T_i(n)] \subseteq F\text{-}TIME[T_i(n) \cdot \log T_i(n)].$$

Proof. The proof is similar to the diagonalization proof in [18]. □

For k-tape Tm's, $k \geqq 2$, we can exploit [36] to get the following result.

COROLLARY 6.12. *For every (total) k-tape Turing machine M_i*

$$TIME_k[T_i(n)] \subseteq F\text{-}TIME_k[T_i(n) \cdot \log^* [T_i(n))].$$

It would be very interesting to see whether the last two results cannot be improved. Unless the result for one-tape Tm's can be improved, it leaves us with the possibility that there can exist sets which are accepted by a Tm M_i running in time $T_i(n)$, but that the best recognition time we can prove in F for these sets is $T_i(n) \cdot \log T_i(n)$. This would be a rather shocking situation.

Note that Theorem 6.5 and Corollary 6.6 yield time bounds for computations which we cannot prove in F, but these are not the actual running times of the Turing machines performing these computations.

The previous results suggest that in the study of different computational complexity measures we should investigate how sharp resource bounds can be proven formally for these measures. A natural measure for the "provability" is given by results analogous to Corollaries 6.10, 6.11 and 6.12. See also [22], [44].

Next we show that if a set A is accepted in time $T_i(n)$ by some one-tape Tm, M_i, then it can be proven in F that such a machine exists, but we do not know whether we can prove for any specific machine accepting A that it runs in time less or equal to $T_i(n)$ (since our best provability result is given by Corollary 6.11).

We first prove a result due to A. Meyer.

LEMMA 6.13. *For any recursive function* $T(n) \geqq n \cdot \log n$

$$\{L(M_i) | T_i(n) \leqq T(n)\} = \{L(M_j) | \vdash_F T_j(n) \leqq T(n) \text{ a.e.}\}.$$

Proof. We construct a recursive function τ such that for all i,

1. $L(M_{\tau(i)}) =$ **if** $T_i(n) \leqq T(n)$ **then** $L(M_i)$ **else** $L(M_{\tau(i)})$ is finite
2. $\vdash_F [T_{\tau(i)}(n) \leqq T(n)$ a.e.]

The machine $M_{\tau(i)}$ has a much larger tape alphabet than M_i so that it can simulate M_i in time $\frac{1}{4}T_i(n)$. $M_{\tau(i)}$ operates as follows:

On input w, $|w| = n$, $M_{\tau(i)}$ lays off $\log^3 n = \log\log\log n$ tape and tries to find on this tape a z, $|z| \leqq \log^3 n$, such that

$$T_i(|z|) > T(|z|).$$

If such a z is found, then the input w is rejected. If not then $M_{\tau(i)}$ simulates M_i on w and accepts iff M_i accepts w.

It is easily seen that $M_{\tau(i)}$ satisfies condition 1; furthermore, $T_{\tau(i)}(n) \leqq T(n)$ a.e., and since we can prove elementary facts about Tm's in F, we can choose a simple construction for τ such that it is provable in F that

$$T_{\tau(i)}(n) \leqq T(n) \quad \text{a.e.},$$

where $T(n)$ is given by some Tm. Note again that the proof of $T_{\tau(i)}(n) \leqq T(n)$ a.e. does not depend on knowing that $T(n)$ is a total function. □

THEOREM 6.14. *For one-tape Turing machines, for any recursive* $T(n)$, $T(n) \geqq n \log n$, *we have*

$$TIME[T(n)] = \{L(M_i) | \vdash_F (\exists M_s)[L(M_s) = L(M_i) \text{ and } T_s(n) \leqq T(n)]\}.$$

Proof. The previous result showed that for every $M_{\tau(i)}$ we can prove in F that

$$T_{\tau(i)}(n) \leqq T(n) \quad \text{a.e.}$$

Therefore we can prove in F that there exists some Tm equivalent to $M_{\tau(i)}$ which runs in time $T(n)$ everywhere by means of a table look-up for the initial input values. □

It follows from Theorem 6.14 that if A can be accepted in time $T(n)$, then there is a formal proof that there exists a Tm which accepts A in time $T(n)$. Though we know from Theorem 6.5 that for many time bounds $T(n)$ and any formal system F there are sets which are acceptable in time $T(n)$, but for no Tm accepting these sets can it be shown that they run in time $T(n)$. This shows an interesting difference in what can be formally proven about the existence of time bounds without being able to prove these bounds for any specific Tm.

COROLLARY 6.15. *There exist monotonically increasing, arbitrarily large recursive functions $T(n)$ such that*

$$\{L(M_i) \mid \vdash_F T_i(n) \leqq T(n)\}$$

$$\subsetneqq \{L(M_i) \mid \vdash_F (\exists M_s)[L(M_s) = L(M_i) \text{ and } T_s(n) \leqq T(n)]\}.$$

Proof. The corollary follows directly from Theorems 6.5 and 6.14. □

Next we consider the problem of program optimization among provably equivalent programs as investigated by P. Young in [44].

In the first part of this chapter we saw that for many resource bounds the corresponding complexity classes and provable complexity classes differed, i.e.

$$F\text{-}TIME[T(n)] \subsetneqq TIME[T(n)],$$

and that gaps occurred in the hierarchy of complexity classes only when the provable complexity classes differed from the nonconstructively defined complexity classes. Thus showing that the complexity results change when we insist that the running times must be provable.

Similarly, in the traditional view of computational complexity we consider all programs computing the same function as equivalent, though we have no way of verifying this; and we know that in any fixed formal system F many of these programs cannot be proven equivalent. Thus we should expect that the results about optimality of all programs computing the same function as a given program will differ from the optimality results about all programs which can be formally proven to be equivalent to the given program. The surprising thing is how much the classical optimization results differ from the optimization results for provably equivalent programs. The most jarring result in this area is that the existence of speed-up among provably equivalent programs is independent of the function computed and depends only on the representation of the program defining the function [7], [44].

For the sake of simplicity we will use the amount of tape as our computational complexity measure and assume that the formal system F has the same properties as postulated earlier in this chapter.

It should be pointed out that we can prove these results for all abstract computational complexity measures for which we can prove the basic complexity axioms in F, namely, if $\{(\phi_i, \Phi_i)\}$ is an abstract computational complexity measure [7], [22], then we must have that

$$\vdash_F (\forall i)[\text{domain } \phi_i = \text{domain } \Phi_i]$$

and

$$\vdash_F [\text{the relation } \Phi_i(x) \leqq n \text{ is decidable}].$$

For more details about provable complexity measures see [17], [44].

It is easily seen that the tape measure (with a minor modification to avoid cycling on finite amounts of tape) satisfies these axioms for any reasonable F.

We furthermore assume that the recursion theorem [38] is provable in F, i.e.,

$$\vdash_F [\rho \text{ is total}]$$

and

$$\vdash_F [\text{if } M_i \text{ total then } M_{M_i[\rho(i)]} = M_{\rho(i)}].$$

We now show that for any Tm M_i we can effectively construct an equivalent Tm, $M_{\sigma(i)}$, which is almost as economical as any Tm probably equivalent to M_i.

LEMMA 6.16. *There exists a recursive function σ such that for any M_i*

1) $L(M_i) = L(M_{\sigma(i)})$;

2) *if* $\vdash_F [L(M_i) = L(M_j)]$ *then for some* $c > 0$, $L_{\sigma(i)}(n) \leqq cL_j(n)$ *a.e.*

Proof. For the sake of simplicity we assume that $L_i(n) \geqq n$. This restriction can be removed at the expense of a somewhat more complicated proof.

For a given M_i we can recursively enumerate all the M_{j_t} such that

$$\vdash_F L(M_i) = L(M_{j_t}),$$

let $M_{j1}, M_{j2}, \dots$ be such an enumeration. Define $M_{\sigma(i)}$ as follows:

Step 0. On input w, $M_{\sigma(i)}$ uses $|w|$ tape squares to list as many $M_{j1}, M_{j2}, \dots$ as possible, say $M_{j1}, M_{j2}, \dots, M_{jk}$. Go to Step 1.

Step n, $n \geqq 1$. On $|w| + n - 1$ tape squares, $M_{\sigma(i)}$ simulates successively

$$M_i, M_{j1}, M_{j2}, \dots, M_{jk}$$

(without exceeding $(|w| + n - 1)$-tape or cycling on a finite amount of tape) until a simulation is completed, whose result is then used as output.

If no simulation can be completed, then go to Step $n + 1$.

It is easily seen (from the assumption that F is sound) that

$$L(M_{\sigma(i)}) = L(M_i)$$

and that for any M_{j_t} there exists a constant $c>0$, depending on the size of the tape alphabets of $M_{\sigma(i)}$ and M_{j_t}, such that

$$L_{\sigma(i)}(n) \leqq cL_{j_t}(n) \quad \text{a.e.},$$

as was to be shown. □

We note that we may not be able to prove in F that $M_{\sigma(i)}$ is equivalent to M_i and it can be shown that in general this cannot be done in F [44].

The next result shows that for any M_i we can effectively construct an equivalent M_{i_0} such that no M_{j_t} provably equivalent to M_{i_0} can use "substantially" less tape than M_{i_0}.

THEOREM 6.17. *For every M_i we can effectively find an equivalent M_{i_0} such that*

1) *$L_{i_0}(n) \leqq cL_i(n)$ a.e. for some $c>0$;*
2) *if $\vdash_F [L(M_{i_0}) = L(M_j)]$ then for some $c>0$, $L_{i_0}(n) \leqq cL_j(n)$ a.e.*

Proof. Let $M_{j_1}, M_{j_2}, \ldots$ be an enumeration of the Tm's provably equivalent to $M_{\sigma(i)}$ from Lemma 6.16. Let $j_0 = \sigma(i)$; thus $M_{j_0} = M_{\sigma(i)}$.

Let the recursive function f, which yields $M_{f(i)}$, be defined as follows:

1. For input w, $M_{f(i)}$ uses $|w|$-tape to enumerate and list as many as possible of the provably equivalent programs to M_i, say, $M_{j_1}, M_{j_2}, \ldots, M_{j_k}$.
2. Search for a minimal $L_{j_t}(w)$ among $L_{j_0} = L_{\sigma(i)}, L_{j_1}, L_{j_2}, \ldots, L_{j_k}$ using as little tape as possible. Let $L_{j_t}(w)$ be this minimum and set

$$M_{f(i)}(w) = M_{j_t}(w) + t.$$

The function f is provably total and therefore we can effectively find a fixed point i_0 such that

$$L(M_{f(i_0)}) = L(M_{i_0}).$$

But then, because of the soundness of F, we must have chosen $j_t = j_0$ and therefore we have

$$L(M_{i_0}) = L(M_{f(i_0)}) = L(M_{j_0}) = L(M_{\sigma(i)}).$$

Furthermore, for any $t \geqq 1$ for which

$$\vdash_F [L(M_{f(i_0)}) = L(M_{i_0}) = L(M_{j_t})]$$

we must have that

$$L_{j_t}(|w|) \geqq L_{j_0}(|w|) \quad \text{a.e.}$$

But from the construction of $M_{f(i_0)}$ it can be seen that for any M_{j_t} there exists a constant c, $c>0$, such that

$$cL_{j_t}(|w|) \geqq L_{f(i_0)}(|w|) \quad \text{a.e.}$$

This concludes the proof. □

A somewhat more complicated proof [44], which we will not give in this paper, shows that for any M_i we can also effectively pick an equivalent M_{i_0} such that every M_j provably equivalent to M_{i_0} has a provably equivalent program which uses a "lot" less tape than M_j and this can be proven in F.

We state just a special case of the more general result [44].

THEOREM 6.18. *For every M_i we can effectively find an equivalent M_{i_0} such that if*

$$\vdash_F L(M_{i_0}) = L(M_j)$$

then there exists a j_0 such that

$$\vdash_F L(M_j) = L(M_{j_0})$$

and

$$\vdash_F L_j(n) \geqq 2^{L_{j_0}(n)} \quad a.e.$$

Proof. See [44]. □

The two previous results jointly show that the speed-up property for provably equivalent programs is independent of the function computed and depends only on the programs describing the computation. Thus we have shown that these results differ radically from the classic (nonconstructive) speed-up results [7], [22].

CHAPTER 7

Relativized $P = NP$ Problem

As stated in the first part of this monograph, one of the most important open problems in computational complexity is to determine the containment relations between the families of languages

$$L, \quad NL, \quad P, \quad NP \quad \text{and} \quad PTAPE.$$

Among these, the most important one is the "classic"

$$P \stackrel{?}{=} NP$$

problem. This problem has attracted considerable attention and it is very likely that its solution will be an important step in our further understanding of feasible computations.

In this chapter we consider the possibility that this famous problem may not be solvable in a formalized mathematical theory, such as set theory. We show that for any fixed axiomatizable formal mathematical theory F, for which Turing machines form a model, there exists a relativized version of the $P = NP$ problem which cannot be proved or disproved in F. A somewhat surprising fact is that we can always choose the relativizing "oracle" set to be the empty set in this *independence* result. This result was obtained independently by T. Baker and in [23].

DEFINITION. For a set A let M_j^A denote the Tm M_j with oracle set A. Correspondingly, let $L(M_j^A)$ denote the set accepted by M_j^A and $T_j^A(n)$ the maximal running time of M_j^A on inputs of length n.

DEFINITION. Let

$$P^A = \{L(M_i^A) | T_i^A(n) \leqq n^k, k = 1, 2, 3, \ldots\},$$

$$NP^A = \{L(M_i^A) | M_i^A \text{ nondet. and } T_i^A(n) \leqq n^k, k = 1, 2, 3, \ldots\}.$$

The following relativization result was obtained in [2].

THEOREM 7.1. *There exist recursive sets A and B such that*

$$P^A = NP^A \quad \textit{and} \quad P^B \neq NP^B.$$

This result shows that the classic $P = NP$ problem cannot be generalized too much; once we permit recursive oracles, the problem disappears. This is a very interesting comment on the nature of one of the outstanding open problems in computational complexity theory. The mathematicians' basic instinct of generalizing destroys this problem, and probably many other problems in computer science are of this type. It furthermore shows that the $P = NP$ problem cannot be resolved by methods which also work for the relativized problems.

Thus a solution of this problem has to deal with the specific properties of polynomial time Turing machine computations, and at the present we seem to lack the necessary techniques to solve it.

It is interesting to note that for random access machines with multiplication ($MRAM$) the deterministic and nondeterministic polynomial time computations coincide [25]. Thus we are provided with a reasonably simple (though not necessarily realistic) model of computers for which

$$MRAM\text{-}P = MRAM\text{-}NP.$$

THEOREM 7.2. *For any formal mathematical system F (satisfying the above assumptions) we can effectively construct a Tm M_i such that $L(M_i) = \varnothing$ and neither*

$$P^{L(M_i)} = NP^{L(M_i)} \quad \textit{nor} \quad P^{L(M_i)} \neq NP^{L(M_i)}$$

can be proven in F.

Proof. Let B and C be recursive sets such that

$$P^B = NP^B \quad \text{and} \quad P^C \neq NP^C.$$

Let the Tm $M(\ ,\ )$ be defined by

$M(x, j) =$ **if** among the first x proofs in F there is a proof that "$P^{L(M_j)} = NP^{L(M_j)}$" and $x \in C$ or there is a proof that "$P^{L(M_j)} \neq NP^{L(M_j)}$" and $x \in B$, **then** accept input **else** reject.

By the Smn theorem there exists a recursive σ such that

$$M_{\sigma(j)}(x) = M(x, j).$$

By the recursion theorem there exists i_0 such that

$$M_{i_0}(x) = M_{\sigma(i_0)}(x).$$

Thus

$$M_{i_0}(x) = M(x, i_0).$$

If there is a proof in F that

$$P^{L(M_{i_0})} = NP^{L(M_{i_0})},$$

then the set accepted by M_{i_0} differs at most finitely from C, and hence we know that

$$P^{L(M_{i_0})} \neq NP^{L(M_{i_0})}.$$

Similarly, if there is a proof in F that

$$P^{L(M_{i_0})} \neq NP^{L(M_{i_0})},$$

then the set accepted by M_{i_0} differs at most finitely from B and hence

$$P^{L(M_{i_0})} = NP^{L(M_{i_0})}.$$

Since we assume that F is sound (i.e., only true theorems can be proven in F), we conclude that there can be no proof of either

$$P^{L(M_{i_0})} = NP^{L(M_{i_0})} \quad \text{or} \quad P^{L(M_{i_0})} \neq NP^{L(M_{i_0})}$$

in F. Thus whether or not

$$P^{L(M_{i_0})} = NP^{L(M_{i_0})}$$

is a question which is independent of the formal mathematical system F. Furthermore, since neither $P^{L(M_{i_0})} = NP^{L(M_{i_0})}$ nor $P^{L(M_{i_0})} \neq NP^{L(M_{i_0})}$ is provable in F we see from the definition of M_{i_0} that

$$L(M_{i_0}) = \varnothing,$$

as was to be shown. □

It should be pointed out that though we knew that $L(M_{i_0}) = \varnothing$ and therefore

$$P^{L(M_{i_0})} = P \quad \text{and} \quad NP^{L(M_{i_0})} = NP,$$

it does not follow that neither

$$P = NP \quad \text{nor} \quad P \neq NP$$

is provable in F. All we have proven is that the particular formulation of the classic $P = NP$ problem in terms of $P^{L(M_{i_0})}$ and $NP^{L(M_{i_0})}$ cannot be resolved in F.

It is interesting to note that if there exists an polynomial time algorithm for the CNF–SAT problem, then for some Tm, M_{j_0}, which solves this problem in polynomial time it is provable in F that $T_{j_0}(n) \leqq n^k$, for some integer k. On the other hand, there may be no proof in F that M_{j_0} solves the conjunctive-normal form satisfiability problem (i.e., that M_{j_0} is equivalent to some well known Tm which solves CNF–SAT).

For the sake of completeness, we exhibit an algorithm which cannot be analyzed in the sense that its running time is independent of the axioms of F. Blum's speed-up theorem [7], [22] shows that there are functions with no best algorithm. What we are saying is something entirely different. There are algorithms with definite running times which are not provable in set theory. In particular we will exhibit an algorithm which runs in time n^2, but for which there is no proof in F of an upper bound less than 2^n, nor is there a proof in F of a lower bound greater than n^2. It is also interesting to compare this result to the results of the previous chapter, where for a very special time bound $T(n)$ (not a running time) we showed that there exist sets accepted in $T(n)$ steps but such that for no Tm accepting this set can it be proven in F that it runs in $T(n)$ or fewer steps.

LEMMA 7.3. *Given the formal system F we can effectively exhibit an i_0 such that the halting of the Tm M_{i_0}, when started on blank tape, cannot be proved or disproved in F.*

Proof. Let $M_i(-)$ denote the Tm M_i with blank input tape. Define

$M(x, j) =$ **if** there is a proof in F that $M_j(-)$ diverges **then** halt **else** diverge.

Again by the Smn and recursion theorems there exist σ and i_0 such that

$$M(x, j) = M_{\sigma(j)}(x)$$

and

$$M_{i_0}(x) = M_{\sigma(i_0)}(x).$$

By a meta argument we conclude that $M_{i_0}(-)$ does not halt, since if $M_{i_0}(-)$ halts, then there cannot be a proof in F that M_{i_0} diverges, which is the only way $M_{i_0}(-)$ can halt. Thus there is no proof in F that $M_{i_0}(-)$ does not halt, nor can there be a proof in F that it does halt. □

We already knew of the existence of the i satisfying the last theorem. A proof in F for each i that M_i did or did not halt would imply that $\{i|M_i(-)\Uparrow\}$ is recursive. What the lemma shows is that we can effectively exhibit a specific Turing machine which does not halt on blank tape but for which there is no proof of this fact in F.

We now show that some algorithms with well defined running times cannot be analyzed in F.

To reveal the simplicity of this proof we make an additional assumption about the formal system F, as described below. This assumption is not essential for the next result, but without it our proofs become considerably longer, since we have to show that the application of Smn and recursion theorems in this proof do not change the running times of algorithms drastically. This can be done, but for the sake of brevity, we are omitting this longer proof.

For any j let $M_{\rho(j)}$ be a Turing machine which, for input w, $|w| = n$, simulates $M_j(-)$ for n steps and if $M_j(-)$ has not halted in n steps $M_{\rho(j)}(w)$ halts in exactly n^2 steps; if $M_j(-)$ does halt in n steps, then $M_{\rho(j)}(w)$ halts in exactly 2^n steps.

We *assume* that there is a construction ρ, as described above, such that we can prove in F for all j that:

$$M_{\rho(j)} \text{ runs in time} < 2^n \quad \text{iff} \quad M_j(-) \text{ does not halt.}$$

THEOREM 7.4. *There exists a Tm M_i (which can be explicitly given) such that*

$$T_i(n) \leqq n^2,$$

but there is no proof in F that

$$T_i(n) \leqq 2^n.$$

Proof. Let i_0 be an index such that $M_{i_0}(-)$ does not halt and for which there is no proof in F that $M_{i_0}(-)$ does not halt; our previous lemma guarantees that we can effectively obtain such an i_0. Then, from our assumptions about F, it follows that there is no proof in F that $M_{\rho(i_0)}$ runs in time $<2^n$, since this would prove in F that $M_{i_0}(-)$ does not halt. Thus $M_\rho(i_0)$ is an algorithm running in time n^2 for which there is no proof in F that it runs in time less than 2^n. □

Next we show that simple problems about context-free languages are independent of the axioms of F, provided we can prove in F elementary facts about context-free languages.

THEOREM 7.5. *One can exhibit a context-free grammar G such that $L(G)=\Sigma^*$ but for which there is no proof in F that $L(G)=\Sigma^*$ or that $L(G)\neq\Sigma^*$.*

Proof. Using standard techniques [27] we can construct for every i a G_i such that $L(G_i)=\Sigma^*$ iff $M_i(-)$ does not halt. Furthermore, if F is sufficiently rich, a proof in F that $L(G_i)$ does or does not equal Σ^* can be extended to a proof in F that M_i does or does not converge. But then using the i_0 for which there is no proof that $M_{i_0}(-)$ converges or diverges, we get a G_{i_0} such that $L(G_{i_0})=\Sigma^*$, but there is no proof in F that $L(G_{i_0})=\Sigma^*$ or that $L(G_{i_0})\neq\Sigma^*$. □

COROLLARY 7.6. *One can exhibit a specific recursive function t such that the equality of the time complexity classes $TIME[t]$ and $TIME[t^2]$ is independent of F.*

Proof. The proof is similar to the previous proof. □

References

[1] A. V. AHO, J. E. HOPCROFT AND J. D. ULLMAN, *The Design and Analysis of Computer Algorithms*, Addison-Wesley, Reading, MA, 1974.

[2] T. BAKER, J. GILL AND R. SOLOVAY, *Relativizations on the P = ?NP Question*, SIAM J. Comput., (1975), pp. 431–442.

[3] L. BERMAN, *Polynomial reducibilities and complete sets*, Ph.D. dissertation, Cornell Univ., Ithaca, NY, May 1977.

[4] L. BERMAN AND J. HARTMANIS, *On isomorphisms and density of NP and other complete sets*, SIAM J. Comput., 6 (1977), pp. 305–323.

[5] ———, *On polynomial time isomorphisms of complete sets*, Proceedings of Theoretical Computer Science 3rd GI Conference (March 1977), Lecture Notes in Computer Science, vol. 48, Springer-Verlag, New York, 1977, pp. 1–15.

[6] P. BERNAYS AND A. A. FRAENKEL, *Axiomatic Set Theory*, North-Holland, Amsterdam, 1958.

[7] M. BLUM, *A machine-independent theory of the complexity of recursive functions*, J. Assoc. Comput. Mach., 14 (1967), pp. 322–336.

[8] M. BLUM AND I. MARQUES, *On complexity properties of recursively enumerable sets*, J. Symbolic Logic, 38 (1973), pp. 579–593.

[9] A. B. BORODIN, *Computational complexity and existence of complexity gaps*, J. Assoc. Comput. Mach., 19 (1972), pp. 158–174.

[10] A. K. CHANDRA AND L. J. STOCKMEYER, *Alternations*, Proceedings of IEEE 17th Annual Symposium on Foundations of Computer Science (Oct. 25–27, 1976), pp. 98–108.

[11] S. A. COOK, *The complexity of theorem proving procedures*, Proceedings 3rd Annual ACM Symposium on Theory of Computing (May 1971), pp. 151–158.

[12] E. CORDOVA, R. LIPTON AND A. R. MEYER, *Exponential tape complete problems for Petri nets and commutative semigroups; Preliminary report*, Proceedings ACM Eighth Annual Symposium on Theory of Computing (May 3–5, 1976), pp. 50–54.

[13] S. EVEN AND R. E. TARJAN, *A combinatorial problem which is complete for polynomial space*, Proceedings Seventh Annual ACM Symposium on Theory of Computing (May 5–7, 1975), pp. 66–71.

[14] M. J. FISCHER AND M. O. RABIN, *Super-exponential complexity of Pressburger arithmetic*, SIAM-AMS Proceedings, vol. 7, American Mathematical Society, Providence, RI, 1974, pp. 27–41.

[15] P. C. FISCHER, *Theory of provable recursive functions*, Trans. Amer. Math. Soc., 117 (1965), pp. 494–520.

[16] J. GILL AND M. BLUM, *On almost everywhere complex recursive functions*, J. Assoc. Comput. Mach., 21 (1974), pp. 425–435.

[17] D. GORDON, *Complexity class of provable recursive functions*, unpublished manuscript, Feb. 1977.

[18] J. HARTMANIS, *Computational complexity of one-tape Turing machine computations*, J. Assoc. Comput. Mach., 15 (1968), pp. 339–352.

[19] ———, *On effective speed-up and long proofs of trivial theorems in formal theories*, Rev. Française Automat. Informat. Recherche Opérationelle Informatique Théorique, 10 (1976), pp. 29–38.

[20] ———, *Relations between diagonalization, proof systems and complexity gaps*, Proceedings Ninth Annual ACM Symposium on Theory of Computing (May 2–4, 1977), pp. 223–227.

[21] ———, *On log-tape isomorphisms of complete sets*, Tech. Rep. TR 77-318, Dept. of Computer Sci., Cornell Univ., Ithaca, NY, July 1977; Theoret. Comput. Sci., to appear.

[22] J. HARTMANIS AND J. E. HOPCROFT, *An overview of the theory of computational complexity*, J. Assoc. Comput. Mach., 18 (1971), pp. 444–475.

[23] ———, *Independence results in computer science*, ACM SIGACT News, 8 (1976), no. 4, pp. 13–24.

[24] J. HARTMANIS AND H. B. HUNT, III, *The LBA problem and its importance in the theory of computing*, SIAM–AMS Proceedings, vol. 7, American Mathematical Society, Providence, RI, 1974, pp. 1–26.

[25] J. HARTMANIS AND J. SIMON, *On the structure of feasible computations*, Advances in Computers, Morris Rubinoff and Marshall C. Yovits, eds., Academic Press, New York, 1976, pp. 1–43.

[26] F. C. HENNIE AND R. E. STEARNS, *Two-tape simulation of multi-tape Turing machines*, J. Assoc. Comput. Mach., 13 (1966), pp. 533–546.

[27] J. E. HOPCROFT AND J. D. ULLMAN, *Formal Languages and Their Relation to Automata*, Addison-Wesley, Reading, MA, 1969.

[28] N. D. JONES, *Space-bounded reducibility among combinatorial problems*, J. Comput. System Sci., 11 (1975), pp. 68–85.

[29] N. D. JONES AND W. T. LAASER, *Problems complete for deterministic polynomial time*, Theoret. Comput. Sci., 3 (1977), pp. 105–117.

[30] N. D. JONES, Y. E. LIEN AND W. T. LAASER, *New Problems complete for log space*, Math. Systems Theory, 10 (1976), pp. 1–17.

[31] R. M. KARP, *Reducibility among combinatorial problems*, Complexity of Computer Computations, R. E. Miller and J. Thatcher, eds., Plenum Press, New York, 1972, pp. 85–104.

[32] R. E. LADNER, *On the structure of polynomial time reducibility*, J. Assoc. Comput. Mach., 22 (1975), pp. 155–171.

[33] N. LYNCH, *On reducibility to complex or sparse sets*, Ibid., 22 (1975), pp. 341–345.

[34] K. MANDERS AND L. ADLEMAN, *NP-complete decision problems for quadratic polynomials*, Proceedings Eighth Annual ACM Symposium on Theory of Computing (May 3–5, 1976), pp. 23–29.

[35] Y. MATIJASEVIC, *Enumerable sets are diophantine*, Dokl. Acad. Nauk. SSSR, 191 (1970), pp. 279–282. (In Russian.)

[36] W. J. PAUL, *On time hierarchies*, Proc. Ninth Annual ACM Symposium on Theory of Computing (May 2–4, 1977), pp. 218–222.

[37] D. A. PLAISTED, *Some polynomial and integer divisibility problems are NP-hard*, IEEE 17th Symposium on Foundations of Computer Science (Oct. 25–27, 1976), pp. 264–267.

[38] HARTLY, ROGERS, JR., *Theory of Recursive Functions and Effective Computability*, McGraw-Hill, New York, 1967.

[39] W. J. SAVITCH, *Relationship between nondeterministic and deterministic tape complexities*, J. Comput. System Sci., 4 (1970), pp. 177–192.

[40] T. J. SCHAEFER, *Complexity of decision problems based on finite two-person perfect-information games*, Proceedings Eighth Annual ACM Symposium on Theory of Computing (May 3–5, 1976), pp. 41–49.

[41] L. J. STOCKMEYER, *The complexity of decision problems in automata theory and logic*, Project MAC, Rep. MACTR-133, Mass. Inst. of Tech., Cambridge, MA, July 1974.

[42] L. J. STOCKMEYER AND A. R. MEYER, *Word problems requiring exponential time: Preliminary report*, Proceedings Fifth Annual ACM Symposium on Theory of Computing (April 1973), pp. 1–9.

[43] C. WRATHALL, *Rudimentary predicates and relative computations*, SIAM J. Comput., 7 (1978), pp. 194–209.

[44] P. YOUNG, *Optimization among provably equivalent programs*, J. Assoc. Comput. Mach., 24 (1977), pp. 693–700.